Collecting
ANTIQUE BIRD DECOYS

An Identification and Value Guide

by

Carl F. Luckey

BOOKS AMERICANA
INC

ISBN 0-89689-043-0

DEDICATION

For

J. W. B.

A friend is one who knows you as you are, understands where you've been, accepts who you've become — and still, gently invites you to grow.

Grateful acknowledgement is given to Dick McIntyre of Port Royal, South Carolina for his seemingly tireless effort in educating me to the ways of old decoys and allowing an invasion of his home more than once to photograph his collection. Thanks also to collectors Don Drennon of Birmingham, Alabama and Neal and Patty Clement of Florence, Alabama for their generosity and patience while photographing their decoys.

CONTENTS

INTRODUCTION

There are many ways to approach the idea of collecting decoys. There are dozens and dozens of known carvers and factories. There are, of course, also dozens of species of birds represented, as well as many different hunting areas and major flyways. With this in mind the collector may choose to specialize in one of the areas. For instance, you might wish to concentrate on decoys that are indigenous to the area you live in, a particular species of bird, factory made decoys, etc. Another very satisfying way of collecting is to obtain any decoy within your means that simply pleases you.

There are three major groups of decoys. They are defined as to maker.

1. **Commercially produced** are those decoys carved and painted by hand for sale purposes.
2. **Non-commercially produced** decoys are those produced by a hunter for his own or friends' use and not sold as a rule.
3. **Factory produced** decoys are those made in a commercial facility, usually turned out in great numbers by machine lathes.

In this presentation the first two categories will be lumped together as hand-carved decoys, and factory-made decoys will be treated separately from them. Each section will present detailed discussions of these categories.

Most decoy collectors refer to certain geographic areas where decoys were carved and hunted over as "Schools" of decoy makers. There are probably thirty or more identifiable schools of carvers in the various flyways, but for the purpose of simplification this book will present only about twenty of the major areas or schools wherein the carvers lived and worked. The information and photographs will attempt to give you some basic tools that should enable you to look at a particular decoy and at least identify what part of the country it is from. The discussion and the photographs within each school are chosen to give you construction techniques and painting styles that are typical of that school.

The general information presented in the first pages of the book will provide you with valuable identification data and prepare you for the more technical data included in the discussion of each major school of carvers.

Factory made decoys will be covered in much the same way.

The value information associated with the listing will be presented in ranges and, in many cases, widely varying ranges. The value ranges are given merely as a guide and most of them have been derived from auction catalogs and dealer sales lists. Given the present state of our economy and its result on the entire collectibles market, these values must be treated only as a starting point in the arrival at the value of a particular decoy. In addition, there has not yet been a firmly established secondary market in decoys, although the many auctions and sales occurring these days are beginning to influence the market toward reasonable stability.

When using the value ranges in this book it is incumbent upon the collector to bear in mind several factors, not the least of which is aptly put by my good friend and noted collector of old fishing lures, Clyde Harbin, "The Bass Man": "Nothin' aint worth nothin', 'til somebody wants it." It really doesn't matter what the value placed on it here, if you don't want it the value is academic; if you do, however, you might be willing to pay more than the high end of the value range listed. There are many other factors influencing values. If, for instance, there is a particularly rare and hard-to-find decoy known to exist only in four or five collections and suddenly, however unlikely, a group of twenty to twenty-five is found in an old barn loft and offered for sale at auction the resulting prices realized might be considerably less than the heretofore accepted value.

Marks on the decoy can also affect value and condition can have a heavy influence. The values presented with the listings here are for decoys in good to excellent condition.

There is a tendency for collectors to take a book such as this one and use it as the final authority. That is foolhardy. The collector must use this book in conjunction with his own experience, the word of a trusted dealer, and all the other sources of value information he can get his hands on; dealer lists, periodical articles, sales ads, auction lists, etc. Remember the values listed here are first of all, just one man's opinion and secondly, they are for a given period of time. Delays inherent in publication make the values a valid opinion for a period of time just prior to publication and release of the book.

A SHORT HISTORY OF THE AMERICAN BIRD DECOY

The origin of the decoy as we know it today lies in early American history, but not with the early settlers as might be reasonably assumed. Rather it pre-dates the American pioneer by at least one thousand, perhaps two thousand years. In 1924 at an archeological site in Nevada, the Lovelock Cave excavations yielded a group of decoys beautifully preserved in protective containers. Among this group of decoys were some stuffed skins, but there were eleven totally artificial decoys fashioned of twisted and bundled tule rushes or bullrushes (reeds) and feathers in a startlingly realistic form that is unmistakably that of a Canvasback duck. The careful manner of their storage preserved them for us to enjoy an estimated one to two thousand years later. More importantly, the extreme care the early Indians took in the preservation of their duck decoys suggests the critical importance to them of duck hunting, and the obtaining of the meat of wildfowl must have been an important factor in their survival.

When the first settlers came to western North America their survival was just as dependent upon hunting wild game for food as that of the Indians. It didn't take them long to notice the various methods the Indians used to lure wildfowl within bow and arrow range. They used a little of everything, from piles of rocks to clumps of mud and dead birds to make likenesses of their prey. Quick to seize upon the idea, those early settlers just as quickly improved it. They began to fashion likenesses of their prey out of different materials, ultimately finding that wood was an ideal raw material. Thus the carving of wildfowl decoys was born.

It isn't likely that those early Americans carved a bird likeness and then said, "Ah ha, a decoy". The lures were called many things but the word "decoy" was not yet in their vocabulary. Just when the word did come into common use is not precisely known buts its etymology or origin is known. Its roots are European, in particular Dutch. Decoy is derived from the Dutch word used to describe a cage-like affair into which the birds were driven by hunters in boats. Later domesticated ducks were placed inside to lure unsuspecting wildfowl into it. The name given to this cage was **ende-kooi**. This method was used before the advent of guns in wildfowl hunting.

Up to the middle of the 1800's there was not sufficient commercial demand for decoys to enable the carvers to make a living at selling, so most decoys were made for themselves and friends. The middle of the nineteenth century saw the birth of the "market gunners". These men were in the business of providing markets with the hundreds of thousands of birds necessary to feed the increasing North American population. These hunters, using huge guns and much of the time deploying rigs of hundreds of decoys, killed hundreds of birds of any sort in one outing. There were no game laws at the time and the seemingly inexhaustible supply of wildfowl provided them with a living and the overcrowded and, for the most part, poor emigrant population of the larger eastern seaboard cities with relatively cheap meat. The market hunters and other hunters killed anything that flew, from Red Breasted Robins and Passenger Pigeons to the majestic Heron and Whistling Swan. Their activities are usually associated with the Chesapeake Bay area, but this slaughter was taking place in all the major flyways. The sad result of this indiscriminate destruction of wildfowl is that the coup de grace was administered to many bird species, rendering them extinct. Some others are on the endangered list as a result. A few examples are: the Passenger Pigeon, Labrador Duck and the Heath Hen. The killing of wildfowl for sale was outlawed by the United States Congress with their passing of the Migratory Bird Treaty Act in 1918.

During this period of time many carvers were to begin making a living with their decoys and the first factory-made decoys came into existence. The huge numbers of decoys required to supply the market hunters (who often utilized 500-600 decoys at a time) and the rising numbers of single hunters for sport or sustenance made commercial decoy carving possible.

3

Following the passage of the 1918 act came the demise of the factory decoys of the day. The large numbers of decoys needed by hunters declined because of the act and many of the smaller commercial carvers had ceased to ply their trade by the 1920's. There were a few of these small, one or two-man or family operations that continued to carve birds, and with the great increase in the popularity of sport hunting the commercial carvers soon found the demand for their production rising. Some of these craftsmen continued to work right on up into the 1950's. Today their tradition is carried on by a few truly great contemporary carvers. The latter produce incredibly intricate, life-like birds. The serious contemporary carvers' products have to meet strenuous requirements, making the decoy such that it **could** be hunted over. The prices these carvings command make it unlikely that they will float anywhere but in a competition water tank. What these contemporary carvings represent is that decoy carving is one of the few early American folk arts that has survived into our modern fast-paced times and still being pursued.

THE DECOY COLLECTOR (Hoardbirdens enmassus)

I don't know whether Mike Beno coined the phrase or not, but his reference to *"Hoardbirdens enmassus", a tongue-in-cheek pseudo-scientific name for the decoy collector is both amusing and appropriate.

The genus and species Hoardbirdens enmassus can be found in all habitats, in all sorts of decorated forms and shapes, and tends to erratic migration. Its call is characterized by various chuckles, screams and exclamations in variations of words sounding like "bird", "block", "toller", "stool", "decoy" or "dee-coy". What all these critters have in common is a voracious appetite and their nests are usually overflowing with their prey, the decoy.

The collecting of decoys is growing in great leaps and bounds today but there have been serious collectors around since Joel Barber first wrote about them from a collecting point of view in his 1934 book, **Wild Fowl Decoys.** Barber is acknowledged by collectors as the granddaddy of decoy collecting. After Barber's book the hobby grew fairly slowly with a few new names popping up from time to time over the years since. It seems that his writings unearthed a larger group of afficionados than he himself realized existed. Names like Mackey, Starr, Sorenson and many others have become legendary among collectors. These were among the first to have written extensively about decoys and collecting. Since then many more have come along with excellent scholarly works for collectors. These will be mentioned later as recommended references.

That these writers have taken such pains to document North American decoys and their makers is evidence enough of decoys as a legitimate collectible. There is further overwhelming evidence that they are not only eminently collectible but that they also enjoy a distinguished status as a truly original American folk art. That status is incontestable when you look at the decoy's inclusion in many fine museum collections and the number of auctions, shows and sales annually devoted exclusively to decoys.

Decoys represent a unique form in American folk art history in that they have a property not common in that genre; they were never intended to be pretty. On the contrary, they were first and foremost made to serve a purely utilitarian function — to lure wildfowl within killing distance of the hunter. If the working decoy turned out to be beautifully carved and painted, it probably was simply for the self-satisfaction of the maker's own artistic tendencies. Some contend that the beautiful ones may have been decorated for the individual user rather than the wildfowl hunted. This may be true to some extent now, but because most of the early makers produced them more for their own or friends' use than for commercial advantage, they were probably shaped and painted on the theory that the more they appeared like the real thing, the more effective they would be. Some makers were more adept at this than others.

The earliest collectors were generally sportsmen who appreciated the aesthetics of decoys as well as the fond memories of hunting over them. These feelings ring out in their writings. This is not always so. Indeed, Joel Barber never even hunted wildfowl in his life. His appreciation was solely for the art form and of their importance as American folk art.

One can readily see that there were huge numbers of decoys produced during the heyday of market hunting by both carvers and factories, but they are fast being snapped up by collectors. One thing that should be pointed out is that many of them went the way of firewood or even landfill after the passage of the 1918 Act and there may not be as many around as might be assumed at first thought.

*In an article in Ducks Unlimited magazine, Sept./Oct. 1982, **A Poet, A Painter, A Whittler of Wood,** by Mike Beno.

DICTIONARY OF TERMINOLOGY

The following pages introduce you to terminology you will encounter in the remainder of this book and in dealing with other collectors and sellers. Careful study and constant reference to it will give you a working knowledge of the terminology, hence making it easier to read sales and auction lists and to describe your pieces to other collectors.

Some terminology listed here is elementary and some even obvious, especially to hunters. They are here because many collectors or would-be collectors are not hunters and may not be familiar with the terms.

ANCHOR LINE TIE — These are as varied as the men who carved decoys. There were screw-eyes, leather loops, or simply nails. The makers used whatever was available but some used the same type most of the time, giving the collector another clue as to the origin of a decoy. It should be pointed out here that over the years of use a hunter may have altered or changed the line tie to suit himself.

BALLAST — Some decoy makers used ballast to make the decoy more stable in the water. In some cases the ballast is incorporated into a keel, but most are simply weights attached to the bottom in some manner. A few makers had a distinctive method for attaching them, helping in identifying the decoy. The weights vary from anything heavy lying around, such as pieces of horseshoes or any chunk of metal, to a well made lead or iron casting. Some were attached before painting, some after, and some consisted of molten lead poured into a cavity hollowed out for the purpose by the maker. There was one school in the Mississippi Flyway in which are found decoys with a swing keel with the ballast at the end, much like some small trailerable sailboats use today. Don't forget that many hunters applied their own ballast or weights, or they may have been removed, so it is not always a reliable indicator of maker or school.

BANJO TAIL — A style of carving usually associated with the Virginia Eastern Shore school of carvers and in particular with Ira Hudson. Appears somewhat like the fret of a banjo.

PLATE 1.

6

BATTERY [Boat] — See SINK BOX

BATTERY GUN — See PUNT GUN

BLOCK — A term sometimes used to mean decoy. Apparently this usage is derived from the block of wood a carver begins with in creating a decoy.

BOTTOM BOARD — Many decoys are found with a hollowed-out body and a flat board fitted to the bottom to seal it off and provide a base. The use and sometimes the thickness of a board can be a clue to maker or school in some cases.

BRANDS — A word used to describe a broad spectrum of marks to be found on decoys. They can range from simple carved initials all the way to complicated company logos. For a detailed description of brands, see pages 15 through 21.

CHECKING — This is the cracking of wood due to the natural oils and moisture drying or evaporating over the years.

COMB FEATHER PAINTING — This is a method of painting a decoy wherein the maker will paint the final coat and set the decoy aside to partially dry. When the paint reaches the proper consistency the maker then uses a comb or comb-like instrument to scratch feather patterns into the paint. This gives a very realistic texture to the finished product.

CONFIDENCE DECOY — William Mackey in his **American Bird Decoys** contends that ". . . the only true 'confidence' decoy is a gull decoy". He goes on to give swan decoys some credit to the title. The confidence decoy is truly a decoy of any species of bird that can instill confidence in another bird. Its presence indicates to a game bird that sees it that food is below and the area is safe to feed in. Swans, gulls, crows and herons are good examples of confidence decoys. Their use on or near a duck blind conveys a sense that nothing is amiss below.

CRAZING — This is a term applied to paint that has cracked in a manner that looks somewhat like a mosaic. Very characteristic of old paint.

DOVE TAIL — See "INLETTED"

EYES — The method a maker used to represent eyes on the decoys varied considerably and, in some cases, can be indicative of the maker or the school from which the decoys came. They used glass eyes that were either imported taxidermy eyes or simply the hat pins so popular with the ladies of those days. Sometimes they merely painted the eye on or carved it right into the head. Upholstery tacks, screws, and even 22 caliber shell cases sometimes were used.

FLAT BOTTOM — Exactly as the name implies, this term refers to the bottom of a decoy that has a uniformly flat bottom. See "V-BOTTOM" and "ROUND BOTTOM".

GUNNING SCOW — This was a special sail boat rigged out with hoists and other necessary equipment for deploying the sink box or battery boats. There were three rather famous ones plying the Chesapeake Bay, **The Susquehanna, The North Carolina,** and **The Reckless.** See section on "BRANDS", pages 15 through 21, "PUNT GUN" and "SINK BOX".

HAWK WATCHING — A term describing the head and neck position of a decoy; up and wary.

HOLLOW BODY — Describes the fact that the decoy body is hollowed out. Generally the hollow-bodied decoys are of two-piece construction, but can be three or more.

IN USE REPAINT — See "REPAINT"

INLETTED — This usually refers to a specific method of attaching a head to a decoy body. It is accomplished by the carver fashioning a hole or cavity in the appropriate area of the body and carving the base of the head or neck portion to fit into this receptacle precisely. This renders the decoy much stronger and makes it more resistant to breakage by the natural tendency of many users to pick up the decoy by the head. Although used to a much lesser extent, the method is also occasionally found used to attach wings, bills, and sometimes other parts of a decoy. Use of this construction technique can help to determine the carver or school from which the decoy came. This inletting is usually a modification of a carpenter's mortise and tenon or dove tail joint.

KEEL — Just as in a boat a keel gave the decoy both upright and lateral stability. They were placed on decoys mainly in areas where the waters tended to be rougher than usual, but not limited to those areas by any means. Keels come in all shapes and materials. Most were fashioned as you would expect, of a strip of wood of varying depths placed longitudinally along the bottom of the decoy. The material and style can vary widely, however. There are fixed keels, swinging keels, folding keels, etc., and they can also be a combination of keel and ballast made of metal and/or wood. See "BALLAST".

LOW HEAD — A self-descriptive term describing decoys with little or no neck. The head is either very low or even almost tucked down into the top of the breast.

MARKET GUNNER — The market gunner was a hunter who made his living killing wildfowl for sale at market. For a detailed description of these men and their equipment, read pages 3 through 4 and see "SINKBOX" and "PUNT GUN".

MORTISED — See "INLETTED".

NAIL — A small protrusion situated at the front and top of the tip of the upper mandible or bill of some species of birds.

NARES or NOSTRILS — These are holes, one on either side of the upper mandibles. Some makers represented them with carving, others with paint or not at all. Occasionally the way a maker carves or paints these features is an identifying characteristic.

NECK NOTCH — A term describing a carved depression in the body of a decoy just behind the neck.

PLATE 2. Neck notch or thumbprint carving is evident just behind the head.

O. P. — See "ORIGINAL PAINT".

ORIGINAL PAINT [sometimes abbreviated O.P.] — This refers to a decoy which has the first or original paint that was applied by the maker. The term does not, however, appropriately describe a decoy that has been repainted by its original maker. See "REPAINT".

OVERSIZE — Refers to a decoy having been made in a scale larger than the normal size associated with the species of bird being carved.

PADDLE TAIL — A tail carved in a paddle shape, usually protruding from about the center of the rear end of the body.

PUNT GUN — Also called "Battery Guns", these were the guns used by the market hunters. These formidable guns could kill many, many birds with one shot. A typical punt gun would be twelve feet in overall length with an eight-foot barrel with a 1½ to 2 inch bore and weighing 100 to 125 pounds. They were capable of firing a whole pound of shot at once. Some were even bigger, being double-barrelled.

RAISED WING CARVING — Some decoy makers took pains to carve the body with the wings clearly raised slightly from the body. Typical of pre-1915 decoys by Elmer Crowell. Sometimes called simply "wing carving".

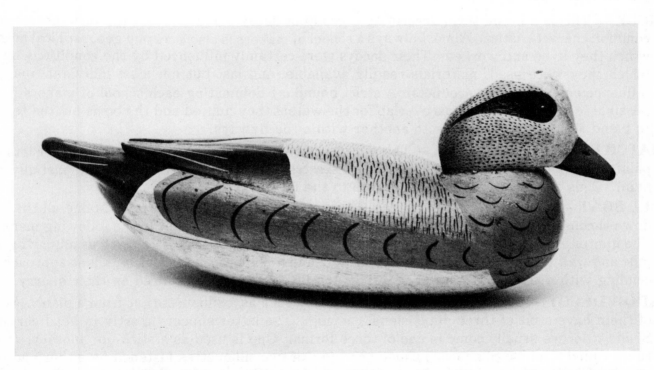

PLATE 3. This Delaware River School drake Widgeon decoy is an excellent example of "Raised Wing Carving".

RECENT REPAINT — see "REPAINT" below.

RE-HEAD — Because the head is the most vulnerable part of a decoy it is the part most usually damaged. So you can readily see that there can be many decoy bodies with heads from another decoy. These are called Re-heads.

REPAINT — There are really three different types of repainted decoys: (1) a repaint done by the original maker, (2) a repaint done by the owner and (3) a repaint done by a professional restorer. Although by far the most desirable repainted decoy is one which has been repainted by the original maker, even it is less desirable than a decoy with the original or first painting by its maker. The user or owner repaint (other than the maker/user) is called a **Working Repaint** or **In-use Repaint** and is the most common condition an old decoy is found in. The third type, the restorer's work, is strictly a matter of owner or potential buyer preference.

RIG — A word used to describe a group of working decoys. The decoys you hunt with are your "rig" of decoys.

RIGGING — This is used to describe everything from the line tie and anchor line down to the anchor.

ROOTHEAD — This is appropriately used to describe decoys with heads made out of a root. Most of the roots were embellished by carving and/or painting, but some were used as is because of natural resemblance to the bird's head.

ROUND BOTTOM — A decoy with a rounded bottom as opposed to a "V-bottom" or "flat bottom", etc., is described as "round-bottomed".

SCHOOL — This is a broad term describing a group of decoy makers whose products share some common characteristics. Almost always a school of makers is also a certain geographical area in which they lived and worked. Their decoys were certainly influenced by the conditions under which they were used, materials readily available, and last but not least individual makers' influence on each others products. A strict boundary delineating each school of makers is not possible to define. The schools overlap for the waters they hunted and the birds hunted tended to blend slowly from one type to another within the flyways.

SCRATCH FEATHER PAINTING — This is a method of feather painting where the maker lets the paint dry somewhat, then comes back and scratches a feather pattern into the partially dry paint. This gives a very realistic texture to the finish.

SCULL BOAT — The scull boat was used all along the Eastern Seaboard from Maine all the way down through the Virginia Eastern Shore. The boat was used to hunt in the following manner: The hunter would deploy his rig of decoys in a likely spot and back off as much as a quarter of a mile and wait for the quarry to spot the rig and land. The boat made a slow, silent approach by sculling with a single oar over the stern of the boat and then they fired on their quarry.

SHADOW DECOY — This is a two-dimensional decoy such as a silhouette cut from a plank. Some of them have a bit of three-dimensional carving. The latter appears mostly in head carving. Shadow decoys usually come in one of three forms. One is used as a stick-up; another, sometimes called "Double Shadows", usually consists of two silhouettes fastened on either end of a couple of strips of wood with six more in various positions nesting in between. The third is illustrated in PLATE 4 on following page.

SHELF or SHELF CARVING — This term refers to a style or characteristic construction wherein the body is carved with a definite rise, making a portion of the bird's neck to receive the head, or head and neck, portion. See PLATE 5, following page.

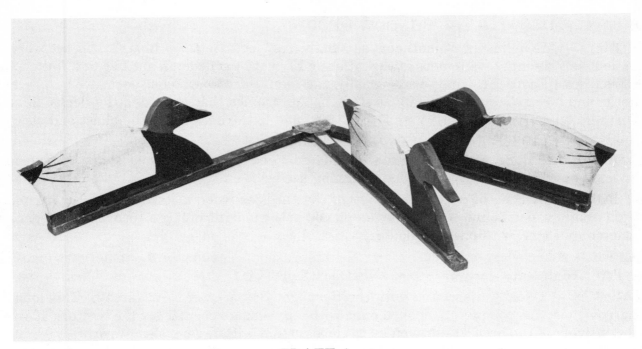

PLATE 4.

PLATE 5. This William T. Shaw drake Pintail from the Illinois River school illustrates the carved shelf made to receive the head and neck.

SILHOUETTE DECOY — See "SHADOW DECOY"

SINK BOX — Also known sometimes as "batteries" or "Battery Boats". These were used extensively by market gunners in the Atlantic Flyway, particularly in, but not limited to, the Chesapeake Bay area. They were usually one-man, narrow wooden boats with very narrow decks and "wings" of wood or canvas stretched on frames that extended the decks all around. On these wings were placed "Wing Ducks" fastened to the deck for both ballast and decoy. The hunter would frequently deploy a 500 to 600 rig of decoys.

The sink box along with the hunter and his gear was deployed by sailboats rigged for this specific purpose. They were called "gunning scows".

SLAT BODY — A type of decoy construction that utilizes wood slats bent over a frame. This lightweight construction was usually employed in the making of large decoys. Some decoys are commonly found with one slat bodies.

SLEEPER — A decoy carved in such a way as to represent a sleeping bird. Sometimes inaccurately called a confidence decoy. See CONFIDENCE DECOY.

SNEAK BOX — Usually associated with the Barnegat Bay area of New Jersey. This long, fairly narrow boat was completely decked over with only a small cockpit for the hunter. It was used extensively in the area. Lightweight in construction with a very shallow draft, it didn't have much weight capacity. This latter factor is said to have influenced the high development of hollow body decoys from that area; ostensibly developed to allow the hunter to carry many more in the sneak box than if they had been made with solid bodies. When the market gunner returned from his hunt he would often have bagged over a hundred ducks.

SOLID BODY — Refers to construction of a decoy body from solid wood as opposed to a hollow body. Generally the solid body will consist of one piece of wood, but they have been found also made of two, three or more laminated layers of wood.

SPLIT TAIL — Some decoy makers carved their decoys more realistically than others. This term refers to the differentiated carving of the tail feathers, showing as definite upper and lower sections. Generally associated with the Delaware River school.

PLATE 6. This Delaware River Canada Goose decoy made by M. L. Perkins illustrates the Split-Tail carving. It could also be described as raised wing carving though this would not be entirely accurate. See "Raised Wing Carving".

STICK-UP — Frequently a decoy was made and mounted to one or more sticks or dowels representing legs (sometimes) that allowed the hunter to stick them into the ground or the bottom of a shallow or marshy area. There have been stick-ups of many species found, but the greatest majority are of shore birds.

STOOL — Once commonly used to describe a single decoy or a rig of decoys. The theory is that the word is derived from the European practice of fastening a live bird, usually a pigeon, to a movable pole or perch called a "stool". One can readily surmise that this also probably gave rise to the phrase "stool pigeon".

STOOLIES — Used to describe dead birds used as decoys.

THUMBPRINT CARVING — See "NECK NOTCH"

V-BOTTOM — Refers to the bottom of a decoy being in a "V" shape, when viewed from front or rear. See "FLAT BOTTOM" and "ROUND BOTTOM".

WATERLINE — A term utilized in describing where the joining of the upper and lower portions of a two-piece construction decoy is located; i.e., "above the waterline" or "below the waterline". The waterline itself is the level at which the decoy floats.

WING CARVING — See "RAISED WING CARVING".

WING DECOY — Usually made of cast iron or lead, these birds were made to serve a special purpose. They were made for use with the Sink Box or Battery Boats utilized by the market gunners as a means of balancing the boat and helping to camouflage the boat by lowering it in the water so that it presented a lower profile. They weighed anywhere from 8 to 40 pounds each, but there have been some found weighing much more. Some were made of wood but they are rarely found. Basically the wooden wing decoy was the upper one-half of a decoy. Some were easily convertible to a regular working decoy by adding an appropriate lower body piece. It can be assumed that this conversion accounts for their short supply. These conversions can be difficult to detect for there were many decoys made with two or three-piece body construction. See "SINK BOX".

PLATE 7. A cast iron Canvasback wing duck.

WORKING REPAINT — See "REPAINT".

COLLECTING DECOYS

The successful and satisfying collecting of anything is not possible without careful study of what you collect, not to mention the possibility of making costly mistakes through ignorance. This book can no more provide you with all you need to know than a hunter can down every bird that passes through his sights, but it can help you get started. The following pages will give you needed information and directions toward a logical learning process.

Any collector who is serious about his particular interest will amass all that is written about it. To this end you will find later on a listing of other books that you need to begin obtaining for your collecting library. In addition to that will be a list of dealers and auction companies that specialize in or at least have moderate selections of decoys for sale.

IDENTIFICATION OF ANTIQUE DECOYS

There are many, many characteristics of decoys that make identification fairly easy in some cases. A considerable number of decoys, for instance, can be identified as to maker by such a simple things as the brand, logo, name or initials. Many makers can be determined because of a certain style or shape. Many of these early craftsmen had very significant styles of carving, construction technique or painting that were unique to the individual maker, making a decoy unmistakably his even in the absence of other identifying marks. This is also true of some of the factory produced birds. For instance some maker's decoys are all of the same distinctive body shape, only painted differently to represent different species of wildfowl. Others had a distinctive style of carving details such as carved delineation of the mandibles and/or carving separating them from the head of the bird. Others used the two-piece hollow construction exclusively or all with heads inletted or all with the upper and lower hollowed-out pieces joined, always above or always below the waterline.

The same type characteristics can be used to at least allow the collector to determine the school or area of the maker most of the time. The list goes on and on, paint styles, painting techniques, method of attaching head to body, position of head, species of bird carved, type of wood used, body shape, size of the decoy, eye types, and shaping of the tail and face carving, etc.

Certain designs are obviously meant to be used in shallow marshes while others are obviously made to be used in deep waters subject to weather.

Knowledge of changing migratory patterns can be helpful also. For instance, if you know that there were few or no Canada geese migrating through the Chesapeake Bay area prior to the 1930's, then you know any Canada goose decoy represented as being from there and dated by the seller as being made by a carver earlier than that is a case of mistaken identification. There would obviously not be any reason for such a decoy to have been made in that area at that time.

This general discussion may lead you to believe it is easy to date and identify the maker of any decoy; not so. True, there are some that are easy to spot and with time and experience gained from the easier identifications you can develop your ability to include identification of more, less obvious examples. The problem is that there are many types of decoy construction as there are opinions of just what constitutes an effective decoy. For the most part, luckily, carvers within a particular school were influenced by the species of bird hunted in his region and by the local conditions under which they had to be hunted. Therefore there **are** common characteristics. The discussion with each school will point these things out. To understand these discussions you must familiarize yourself with the Dictionary of Terminology in the previous pages. I suggest that, if you haven't already, you read through it and then each time you encounter a word or term you don't understand, refer back to the dictionary. This way you should end up with a working knowledge of most of the terms common to collecting decoys.

If you are a beginning collector you shouldn't be afraid of what you will find. There seems to be a tendency among novice collectors to pick up what is truly a fine decoy that has no documentation or provenance, in a shop or fleamarket, and then let it go. This reluctance is understandable, but if it has the look and feel of a good piece, by all means buy it. Many have an inherent ability to recognize good form and design. If you don't have it, you can develop it simply by handling and examining a few that are known quantities. You can sometimes be fooled, but not often, by today's decorative reproductions. More about this will be covered later.

BRANDS

The term "brand" as used in this book, and by most collectors, encompasses just about any markings placed on a decoy (usually on the bottom) by a user, maker or collector.

If a collector places his mark on a decoy it is usually a paper label or a rubber stamp type. There is seldom any doubt as to their marks. This practice is not particularly widespread for just about every good decoy, especially those that are extremely valuable, is known by more than one collector. Each decoy can usually be identified by its own distinctive nicks or wear pattern. Additionally, most of these high-value decoys are documented through auction catalog photography and description.

The remaining two categories of brands must be treated separately. User and maker brands can be very significant in dating a decoy, documenting its maker and influencing its value.

Unfortunately the majority of decoys don't have brands or, at the least, the brand doesn't mean anything. The latter is particularly true in the case of user brands unless the user can be identified and is of historical importance to collectors.

In the case of a decoy on which both user and maker brands appear, each being known and important, you have a real prize. The importance of either or both brands can have a very positive influence on the value of the decoy, especially if the decoy is otherwise insignificant. The value can be increased by two to five times, depending on the brand.

Any type of brand can be confusing to the uninitiated. To them any name found on the bottom of a decoy is thought to be that of the maker. More than once has someone thought that the name on the decoy that "Gramps" used was that of a friend or a hunting buddy who made it. Dealers are confronted with this from time to time.

What follow here are descriptions of some of the most famous and significant maker and user brands that you might find. There are, of course, more than are listed here, but the two lists are of many of those considered most important.

USER BRANDS

A user or owner brand can be that of the individual owner or of a hunting club or lodge. It usually appears in the form of a genuine brand such as those used in the cattle business. It wasn't a particularly expensive proposition in those days to have a local blacksmith fashion a branding iron for the impression of initials or name into a wooden decoy by heated iron or by striking with a hammer. Many owners and makers didn't go to the trouble but simply carved or painted their marks.

From time to time there may be more than one user brand found on a decoy. Whatever the number found, they can be interesting if not significant. For instance, I have seen a Harry Shourds Black Duck decoy with three brands on the bottom: H. W. Cain, B C P, A C. Now the "C" common to all three brands suggests that H. W. might be Grampa, A C might be his son, and B C P could be his grandson. Conjecture, yes, but if so think how exciting it might be for his family to possess this particular bird. Incidentally, this particular decoy was spotted by a collector in someone's front yard being used as a decoration with a heavy coat of chartreuse green. (More about decoys painted like this later.)

15

ACCOMAC was the name of a hunting club in the heart of the Virginia Eastern Shore about 65 miles north of Norfolk. This brand is found mostly on shore birds but also on a lot of good duck decoys. A decoy valued at about $200.00 would bring upwards of $850.00 if the Accomac brand were present.

BARRON is a relatively scarce brand to be found. It is the name of an Eastern Shore Virginia hunting club. It seems that the Barron hunters believed faithfully in the the Mason factory-made decoys for as far as it is known so far the brand has shown up mostly on Mason decoys, but there have been a few very fine, unidentified decoys found bearing the brand as well. The Barron brand on a Mason decoy increases its value by about 50%. When it is present it is usually found in two places, on the back and on the side.

CHATEAU. Fred Chateau was a game warden who lived in Accord, Massachusetts. His brand has shown up on Joe Lincolns and some Martha's Vineyard decoys as well as a good many other New England decoys.

GOOSEVILLE G.C. The Gooseville Gunning Club was another Eastern Shore Virginia club. It went out of existence prior to World War I, so any bird found with this brand can be dated no later than 1917. Most decoys found bearing this brand will bring about twice the normal price for it. For instance, a Dave "Umbrella" Watson Black Buck decoy in good structural condition and good original paint would normally bring about $700.00 to $800.00, but with the Gooseville brand it would be worth about $1500.00 to $2000.00.

HARD. This Hard Gun Club brand is found on many good factory decoys such as Masons, Dodge and Petersons.

NORTH CAROLINA. The North Carolina was one of three well known gunning scows. Each of the sailboat's rig of decoys was branded with the boat's name. As in the case of the other two gunning scows, just about any decoy with the brand would be worth at least $500.00. The **North Carolina** sank in 1888 on the Chesapeake Bay.

N P W. The initials in this brand are those of Nelson Price Whittaker. He was one of those who cast the heavy iron wing decoys for use with sink boxes.

ED PARSONS. Parsons was a legendary market gunner who hunted **only** over decoys made by Ben Dye and Captain John "Daddy" Holly; therefore, if you find a Parsons brand on a bird it is most likely to be one or the other. The brand was a "P" within a circle.

RECKLESS. The Reckless was one of the earliest gunning scows. The brand could make an otherwise insignificant upper Chesapeake Bay canvasback duck decoy in the $50 to $100 range worth $500 easily.

SUSQUEHANNA. The Susquehanna was another of the old gunning scows whose brand makes the decoy worth much more than the norm. Same comments apply here as to the **Reckless** and the **North Carolina**. The **Susquehanna** sank just before the Civil War so, obviously, any decoy branded with its name pre-dates 1860-65.

SUYDAM. This brand belonged to a wealthy Long Island family that did much sport hunting in Long Island Sound. The brand shows up relatively often on good Long Island decoys.

PLATE 8.

MAKER BRANDS

Few of the probably thousands of individuals who carved decoys for personal or commercial purposes identified them with a brand of some sort, but most of the factory-made decoys did carry brands. The factory brands will be covered separately in that section of the book. The listing presented here is of several of the more important makers who sometimes, often, or always identified their decoys with a brand.

The descriptions below are of brands only. The individual characteristics of the carver's products are discussed in the text of the school of carvers he is normally associated with.

MAKER BRANDS (Non-Factory) of Significance

Joel Barber. This is the same Joel Barber we have discussed earlier. He is one of the big names in decoy collecting. After Barber wrote his book **Wild Fowl Decoys** he decided he would try his hand at carving decoys himself. His brand, when present, is very distinctive and readily recognizable. It is represented in PLATE 9 on the following page.

PLATE 9.

PLATE 10. This Redhead made by Joel Barber is branded. It has been said that he once stated that he didn't place the brand (Plate 9) on but eight of his decoys. This bird was made only as an example of what he thought a "modern" (1934) decoy ought to look like.

PLATE 11. A Joel Barber Ring Neck drake made for use as a working decoy. Most of his decoys were made for the aesthetics rather than the utility. This particular decoy was supposedly made for use. Its condition testifies that if it ever was used to hunt over it was well cared for. It bears his hand signature on the bottom where the keel has been removed.

PLATE 12. A Joel Barber Black Duck made very much like a St. Clair Flats decoy with a hollow body and a one-quarter inch bottom board.

Thomas B. Chambers was a carver from the St. Clair Flats area. He did not always place his brand but when he did it is easy to identify. It simply stated "Thomas B. Chambers, Maker" and was stenciled onto the bottom.

Nathan Cobb Family. The Cobb family were originally New Englanders who migrated south to Virginia. Their products are best identified by construction techniques and style, but they sometimes carved their initials into the bird. Since they did not brand but **carved** an initial into their decoys, it is more a matter of interest than anything else. Most of the time you will find only an "N" for Nathan Cobb, an "E" or an "A" carved into their products, if you find any at all. Both are illustrated in Plates 13 and 14.

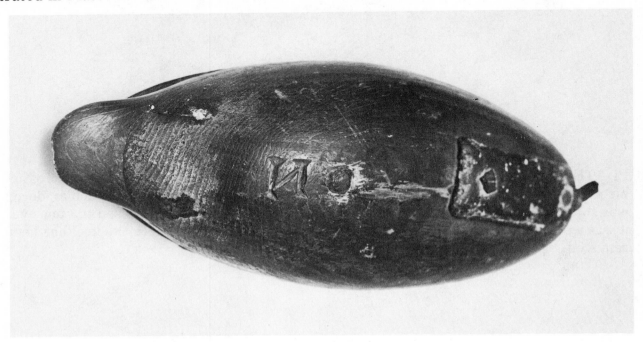

PLATE 13.

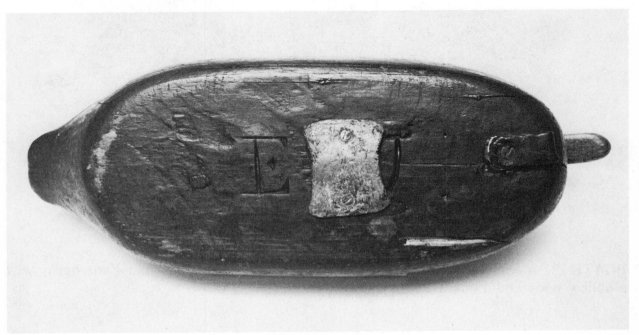

PLATE 14.

Elmer Crowell. The oval brand was customarily used by Crowell starting around 1915 and the rectangular version is usually associated with his later work and/or his son Kleon's work. Unfortunately the decoys carved by Crowell prior to 1915 before he adopted a brand are considered to be his finest work. Collectors should be aware that a few decoys have shown up with an apparently authentic Crowell brand which are known not to be his work.

Lee and Lem Dudley were twins who lived, hunted and carved decoys in the far northern Currituck Sound area of the outer banks of North Carolina. The brand "L. D." found on their decoys could be either brother, although the late Bill Mackey states in his **American Bird Decoys** that most probably it was Lem Dudley who carved most of the decoys. Simplest of the brands to forge, it has been known to happen so it behooves any collector interested in Dudley decoys to get to know their characteristics intimately. Illustrated in Plate 115.

Mitchell Fulcher was also a North Carolina maker. He, like the Dudleys, also identified his decoys with his initials, "M. F."

Laing. Albert Laing decoys are almost always found with his last name branded large and clear on the bottom.

DECORATIVE AND REPRODUCTION DECOYS

A discussion of decorative decoys of the several available types is absolutely necessary in a book devoted to guiding the collector in this hobby. Experienced and seasoned collectors are quite cognizant of these products, but some could very well mislead those who are new to the hobby or at least contemplating beginning a collection of decoys.

Collectively, decorative decoys comprise several types. These are:

(1) Those decoys being carved and painted by craftsmen/artists of great talent. They could be called "Modern Folk Artists".

(2) Reproductions of classic antique decoys. These are almost always offered in a reduced scale from the originals. Some are offered in a "limited edition" and all are (or should be) well well identified as to exactly what they are.

(3) Those decoys factory-made or hand-made that are offered to the public strictly as a decorator item. They have no claim, nor do their makers make any claim, to anything other than that.

(4) Those decoys offered by various companies in kit form for finishing by individual hobbyists or those that are made by individuals for their own use or enjoyment.

The first category is the most important of the four mentioned above. The carvers of these fine bird sculptures, for that is truly what they are, find their progenitors among the early master makers of the working wildfowl decoy. Many of those early makers just weren't satisfied with their product unless it reflected their own high knowledge of the anatomy and habit of the living bird. They were truly artists who couldn't help expressing their talents in the working decoy.

The contemporary carvers are carrying on the active pursuit of this acknowledged original early American Folk Art. It could be said that the competition of today finds its roots in the first organized competition of decoy makers that was held in Bell Port, Long Island, in 1913. Charles E. "Shang" Wheeler, one of the old master decoy makers, entered his work in this competition and walked away The Grand Champion.

Most of these contemporary sculptures in wood are easily recognized by their extreme detail and excellent workmanship. In addition to this attention to anatomical and feather detail, the decoy must also pass a set of strict requirements of floating attitude, etc., taken from both the real birds' habits and those that would be necessary for a working decoy.

A few contemporary carvers do work in the old style as in the accompanying photographic plates.

The second group, that of reproductions, is probably the most controversial among collectors. Many seasoned serious collectors look upon these products with disdain, but the fact remains that they exist and satisfy the appetites of many individuals. They are usually done in a smaller scale than the original and well marked as reproductions. Some are machine made and some entirely hand-made. Like the originals, however, even the machine made likenesses have to have finishing, carving and painting applied by hand.

Third is a group of decoys that are factory-made or hand-made for **decorative purposes** only. The legitimate makers of these decorator items clearly mark their products so that the new collector should have no problem identifying them for what they are. Some are strikingly beautiful and can make wonderful additions to those who decorate their houses with early American style furnishings.

The last category is that of the various individual wood-working hobbyists who either create their own designs or finish factory-made kits that are available in various stages of completion. The finished products in this category can vary from crude to wonderfully detailed decorations, depending on the abilities of the hobbyist.

PLATE 16. A drake Merganser made by contemporary carver Dave B. Hawthorne of Salisbury, Maryland.

PLATE 17. Hen Widgeon by contemporary maker Frank Beck of New Holland, Pennsylvania.

PLATE 18. Drake Widgeon mate to the Frank Beck hen.

It is not unreasonable to assume that there may be some hunters out there who still carve their own working decoys from wood simply for the sheer satisfaction of making their own wooden working decoys in the tradition of their ancestors.

All of the above have a particular market, from the active collector of the beautiful decoys created by contemporary artisans to the kits and individually made decorative decoy. They are not, however, looked upon as a part of decoy collecting. The information is presented more for interest and especially for the neophyte collector so that he may not become confused in the early phases of building a collection and learning about antique decoys.

MISREPRESENTATIONS, FORGERIES AND FAKES

In the course of research for this book I thought it might be interesting if I were to take a day's tour through my own area to see what, if anything, I might turn up in the way of old decoys. I found many types of decorative decoys, all priced fairly reasonably for what they were, one identifiable, rather inferior but decidedly old decoy priced at $80.00, and the last one I found was the most interesting; that is, from the standpoint of what the new collector might occasionally run into. It was a nicely formed and carved decoy with lots of "documentation". There was a large tag attached to it giving its maker's name (unknown to me), its origin (Long Island, New York), dates, etc. The body was graceful and carved nicely but it was battered beyond help. There was also a price tag attached to the neck by a string — $145.00! What makes this so incredible is that the neck and head were made of **plastic**, not to mention the fact that it was in a much-too-large scale for the body. I have no doubt that this antique shop owner accepted the bird in good faith from someone else. It was not **intentionally** misrepresented, but it was nevertheless a misrepresentation. I have no doubt that even the newest "wet-behind-the-ears" collector of old wooden decoys would not likely be taken in by this, but it serves well enough to illustrate a point. You need to study and handle the "real McCoy" before leaping into collecting. It isn't hard nor is it a frightening proposition to learn how to recognize a good vs. a bad decoy in this type of encounter. It is the outright fake or forgery that you need to be aware of.

Fortunately there are few if any nefarious dealers in antique decoys and most antique shop owners and fleamarketeers are honest. The latter two, however, seldom know decoys. These shops and fleamarkets can be good hunting grounds if you know your stuff. You might find a real treasure for just a few bucks.

Using the example of the plastic head above, we come to the problems of "reheads". Don't misunderstand reheads as misrepresentations, fakes or forgeries because the discussion appears here. The majority of old bodies fitted with old heads that are not the originals are legitimate. Remember that bills and heads are usually the part of a decoy most susceptible to damage in handling, so many hunters had to replace heads from time to time. Don't worry about that problem for now. The ability to recognize a rehead most of the time will come with increased familiarity with individual, recognizable characteristics of various makers. Reheads represent an altered form of a decoy, hence its inclusion here.

So far not too many outright fakes or forgeries have reared their ugly heads, but it has happened. A few obviously inferior decoys have been found with the easily recognizable oval brand of Elmer Crowell, and the most popular forged "brand" is that of Lee and Lem Dudley for they simply carved "L. D." into their products. Fakes of Mason decoys have shown up and by far the most popular subjects of forgers are the decoys made by the Ward brothers, Lem and Steve.

So far, so good. Not many of these bogus offerings have turned up but, as in any area of collecting where some of the items have reached values as high as decoys have, we have to be ready for anything. There are many, many exceptionally talented craftsmen in the United States today and it would be safe to say that among them are a few bad apples. In addition, with the spate of well formed decorator decoy bodies and kits for the hobbyist, a dishonest individual wouldn't have to be necessarily endowed with great carving talent, only a degree of ingenuity.

There are many ways to artifically age a paint finish; for instance, I know from experience that it can be done fairly effectively. In the course of preparation for my book **Old Fishing Lures and Tackle** I reproduced a couple of classic bass plugs in my workshop, painted them and "aged" the paint. They would never fool a knowledgeable collector, but the neophyte **might** be taken in by my product. Incidentally, I clearly identified these plugs as to what they were and they have never left my possession. To be on the safe side I am in the process of repainting them with a shiny new paint job so I can fish them.

All of this comes down to one cardinal rule of collecting: Establish a good working relationship with one or more recognized, knowledgeable and trustworthy dealers. I know of none of these dealers who wouldn't back up his sale to you with a guarantee of reimbursement if what he sold you turns out to be other than what he represented the decoy as.

RESTORATION AND REPAIRS

There are always two schools of thought among collectors when the subject of restoration comes up. One is well-labelled the purist approach; that is the strong belief that the decoy should be left "as is", that no restoration effort should be made. Some collectors of this persuasion will, however, approve of taking the years of working repaints down to what is left of the first or original coat. I am of the purist persuasion but would, in the case of my own collection, be among those who would like to take any crude repaints down to the first or second coat, especially in the case of the Harry Shourds black duck discussed on page 15, 62 & 63.

The other group are those who advocate complete or partial restoration. This could run the spectrum actually from a simple paint touch-up to replacing broken or rotten wood parts and faithfully reproducing the style of painting of the original maker.

What you do or think about restoration is strictly a personal decision made under whatever circumstances there are. You should know, however, that probably the majority of serious collectors prefer the decoy to be left as it is. Further, if you do elect to have a decoy restored, it is incumbent upon you to be certain that you say it has been done before selling or swapping the bird. My own opinion goes a step further. Each restored decoy should be clearly and permanently marked as such in an inconspicuous place, preferably on the bottom. That way all subsequent owners will know exactly what has been done to it.

The condition of a decoy is an extremely important consideration when placing a value on it. A restoration of any sort can have a tremendous influence on its value in either direction, so you must think carefully before having any restoration done.

CARE OF YOUR COLLECTION

You might think that just because many of your decoys survived the ravages of water and rough treatment by hunters, you don't have to give them any special consideration in the display or transport of them. No so. If you give it just a little thought, millions of decoys were made and used over the years. There can be no realistic estimate made as to how many have survived, but suffice it to say that they are becoming more and more difficult to find in any condition, much less good to excellent condition.

Any wooden object is subject to a number of different hazards. "Checking", the splitting or cracking of decoys is not an uncommon problem. Some of it is due to the maker not using sufficiently seasoned wood. Due to subsequent drying out of unseasoned wood, checking can and does happen. Consider also that a decoy may have lain untouched for years in a boathouse, shed or barn with more or less constant moisture conditions. You find it, add it to your collection in your modern climate-controlled home, which is very dry as a rule and after some months a crack appears. It could be dismaying, but you can do little about the problem unless you have the wherewithal to install expensive systems like the better museums have. This is a problem most of us will have to accept as inevitable. It doesn't happen often but does nevertheless happen.

There are some precautions you can take to at least retard this problem, and others you can take easily to alleviate the likelihood of damage.

For one thing, make sure that your display is not subjected to direct blasts of heat or cold from a floor or wall register. They look great on a mantel, but if you use your fireplace even just occasionally, don't leave them up there. That is one of the worst places to display them. Heat and smoke will do much harm to your decoys.

Never let them be exposed to direct sunlight even for a few minutes each day. The cumulative damaging effect of ultraviolet light from the sun can fade the already fragile paint. A little known fact is that continuous exposure to fluorescent light can do the same thing. Try to avoid exposure to either one.

There has been some controversy concerning applying oil or wax to a decoy. Once again a purist might not agree because it alters the original state of the decoy. Again this must be an individual decision, but it is known that proper application of these materials to any wood acts as a preservative by "feeding" the wood. You wouldn't hesitate to care for a piece of fine antique furniture in this manner, so why not your decoys? Obviously, rigorous rubbing of an already old and fragile paint job may do it irreversible harm. Judgement enters into the picture in this case.

Not too much has been written about termites, "powder-post" beetles or lyctid beetles and other wood boring insects, but this problem presents a very real and present danger. If they are in the wood, they can not only damage or destroy your decoy but can literally eat your house from around you if they spread to the wood surrounding the infested object.

If you find small piles of fine dust around a decoy, don't panic. Just remove it from your collection and isolate it. Recent research has indicated that freezing the piece of infested wood will usually kill the live lyctid beetles, but not much is yet known about the effect on the larvae of the beetle. My advice would be to freeze it for several days and isolate it for about a month, preferably in a sealed plastic bag or tightly lidded metal box. Inspect it periodically for new evidence of the dust-like, powdery spills from the tiny holes made by the beetle. If no new ones are found, you're probably safe.

A most important consideration in the care of your collection is insurance and theft protection. This can be of paramount importance if your collection has grown for some years and represents a sizable sum of money in appreciated value. Additionally, much of it may be irreplaceable.

There are some safeguards against these threats, not the least of which is insurance. I would bet that a great many collectors are sublimely comforted by the mistaken belief that their home-owners' insurance covers their collection. They are suffering from a common but risky supposition. Most of these policies specifically exclude such collections. This is not the place to go into the complexities of special insurance riders or policies to cover a valuable collection. It does serve to give notice to the collector that the situation should be examined by a trusted insurance expert.

A careful record of your collection is almost obligatory in its protection. If you have a good record of the items in your collection, it can be of immeasurable aid in documenting your loss in the case of loss due to fire, theft, etc. Law enforcement authorities often turn up stolen goods that cannot be claimed by the true owner because of lack of ownership documentation.

As we have already noted, many decoys are documented through auction sales catalog photography and collector familiarity with certain of the more well-known examples. Collector George Ross Star Jr., M.D., in the "Wildfowl Decoys" chapter in **The American Sporting Collector's Handbook*** states on page 49, "Personally, I am always pleased with publication of photos of the better birds in my collection on the premise that the more people who can recognize them the harder it would be to sell any illegally and the more apt they are to be recognized and reported if offered for sale." I strongly agree with Dr. Starr, however caution should be exercised in your choice of publication, if the occasion arises. One collector I know of refuses to be identified as the owner of his birds when photographed for publication, for fear of burglary. This is sensible if he doesn't have a sophisticated and reliable security system for his collection.

*Edited by Allan J. Liu, copyright 1976 by Winchester Press

It is strongly recommended that you accomplish a detailed listing of each decoy in your collection. A very effective method is to photograph each of them and record any distinguishing characteristics on the reverse of the photo, such as species, maker, marks or brands, size, and any readily recognizable wear patterns, nicks, etc. You should keep this in a safe place away from your home such as a bank safe deposit box. If you wish to have such a record in your home for the convenience of making changes and additions, make sure it is a **second** set and be certain that you make the same additions and corrections to the other set in your safe deposit box. With this kind of record, in the event of theft and recovery, you should have no problem reclaiming your decoys. It will also go a long way toward establishing the amount of your loss to insurance companies.

DECOY DEALERS AND COLLECTORS

There are hundreds of collectors around the country some of which are dealers as well. The best way to make contact with many fellow collectors is to obtain a copy of the **National Directory of Decoy Collectors,** edited by Gene and Linda Kangas. You might find it available from a dealer, but you can get a copy direct from them if you wish. The address is 6852 Ravenna Road, Painesville, Ohio 44077.

Aside from the dealer source of decoys there are also the collectors. In the course of collecting decoys many of them will change their tastes or direction of their efforts or simply replace a decoy with another found in better condition. Whatever the reasons often collectors have a few birds they would like to sell or trade. Collectors with anything to sell will probably be glad to provide you with a list upon request. This is certainly true of dealers and for a nominal fee to cover printing and postage they will mail it to you. When writing for information to either group it is always advisable to include a self-addressed stamped envelope (SASE).

When contemplating a purchase it is always best to obtain as detailed a description as possible. Along with this information it is a great help to get a good quality photograph also. Obviously the best way to buy is on the spot after a careful personal examination, but there is no decoy supermarket around the corner from most of us so the mail and the telephone are what we have to use. If, after you have taken all the steps to insure what you are buying is what you get and when you get it it isn't, most dealers will back up their offerings if you can satisfy them that what you bought is not what you thought it was.

Once you have located a few folks you like to deal with hang on to them. Remember the old admonishment, "If you buy furs, know your furrier."

The following list of dealers are well established and have fine reputations. They are recommended as your first contacts when starting a collection of decoys.

Dick McIntyre
608 Old Ford Road
Port Royal, South Carolina 29935

Bob Richardson
Box 433
Cambridge, Maryland 21613

Dan S. Young
Route 1, Box 52
Paradise Island
Awendaw, South Carolina 29429

John Delph
Riverswynd Antiques
465 Union Street
Marshfield, Massachusetts 02050

H. A. Fleckenstein Jr.
Box 279
East New Market, Maryland 21631

Hawthorne House
RFD 6, Box 409
Salisbury, Maryland 21801

Chares T. Ward
2486 Washington Ave.
Oceanside, L.I., New York 11572

Charles F. Murphy
The Sneak Box
Strawberry Banke
P. O. Box 4033
Portsmouth, New Hampshire 03801

Ted Harmon
2320 Main Street
Barnstable, Massachusetts 02630

DECOY AUCTIONS

There are many auctions of old decoys that take place each year in the United States. Most of them are smallish and are held in conjunction with the meetings of various collector organizations or wildfowl festivals, etc. Watch for the dates and places these take place in the publications aimed at decoy collectors and hunters.

There are, in additon to the meetings, some auction companies that devote varying degrees of attention to the auctioning of old American decoys. These companies are listed below along with their addresses. Attendance at these auctions can be an education in itself. It gives the collector a chance to personally examine and handle many different examples of decoys from the hands of dozens of makers representing most of the major schools of makers. You can experience the differences first hand. Another great benefit to be derived from these auction companies is to obtain the auction sales catalogs. The catalogs are heavily illustrated and serve very nicely as identification and documentation manuals for literally hundreds of decoys and related items. Be sure that you get a copy of every sales catalog that is issued by the auction companies whether you are interested in buying or not. Don't forget to include the extra buck or two so that they will send the results of the sale. This will give you a good reference as to value when you need it. These results may not reflect the actual market as accurately as we would want it. Don't forget that the occasion of an auction can be influential on the buyers and actual prices realized can reflect the heat of the moment so to speak. "Auction fever" can do strange things. Keep in mind also that a collector may be in hot pursuit of a particular decoy and be willing to pay a great deal more than the bird is worth, especially if he has any bidding competition from another collector who covets the same bird. What this means simply is that the results may not reflect the true picture, but it is just about all we have to go on. It's going to be a "ball park" figure and a good place to start.

All three of the companies listed below are well known to collectors of just about anything. Each of them holds auctions for many things other than decoys. The reason they are singled out is that all of them do hold special auctions for the sale of old decoys in some quantity. The Bourne company is the king among them as far as most collectors are concerned, with Doyle close on their heels. Sotheby's holds auctions periodically that include fairly sizable lots of decoys.

RICHARD A. BOURNE CO., INC.
P. O. Box 141
Hyannis Port, Massachusetts 02647

WILLIAM DOYLE GALLERIES
175 East 87th Street
New York, New York 10028

SOTHEBY'S
1334 York Avenue
New York, New York 10021

PHILLIPS
867 Madison Avenue
New York, New York 10021

PERIODIC PUBLICATIONS FOR DECOY COLLECTORS

The following is a list of publications that are either devoted exclusively to collecting decoys or contain regularly running features or columns about decoys, their makers or related materials. All contain varying degrees of decoy sales advertising.

DECOY HUNTER
901 North 9th, Clinton, Indiana 47842. Subscription cost is $10.00 per year for six issues.

DECOY WORLD
P. O. Box 1900, Montego Bay Station, Ocean City Maryland.

NORTH AMERICAN DECOYS
Hillcrest Publications, Inc. P. O. Box 246, Spanish Fork, Utah 84660. This is a very high quality magazine that has varied quite a bit in frequency of publication over the years. There are no rates published for a subscription presently but it is highly recommended that the collector write them and have your name placed on their mailing list. There are some back issues available from them and well worth adding to your reference library.

SPORTING CLASSICS
P. O. Box 770, Camden, South Carolina 29020. Subscription cost is $12.00 per year for six issues. This fine magazine carries a regular column about old decoys and regularly runs features about decoys. Covers many different types of sporting collectibles as well.

SPORTING CONNECTION
Londonderry, Vermont 05148. This is a tabloid style newspaper that is published quarterly. Subscription cost is $10.00 per year for the four issues.

WARD FOUNDATION NEWS
The Ward Foundation, Inc., Salisbury State College, Salisbury, Maryland 21801. This is a quarterly magazine published for the members of the foundation. Membership for an individual is $15.00 per year and includes a subscription to the magazine.

RECOMMENDED BOOKS FOR DECOY COLLECTORS

To purchase all the books listed below would represent quite a sizable cash outlay, but each of them is a valuable tool in learning about decoys and their makers. If you collect from all the various schools of makers you will have to make an effort to obtain them all over time. Each of them has indispensable data for collectors. If you specialize in one or two areas you are a bit more fortunate, but even study of areas in which you do not collect can be very helpful. The study of the entire area of decoy collecting is a fascinating and enjoyable task. You may get lucky if you make a trip to your local library. There are, incidentally, some really good books about hunting and American folk art that have good sections on old decoys so don't overlook them in the card catalog.

AMERICAN BIRD DECOYS by William J. Mackey, Jr. Copyright 1965 by William J. Mackey Jr. and reissued by Schiffer Publishing Ltd., Box E, Exton, Pennsylvania 19341.

AMERICAN DECOYS by Quintina Colio. Copyright 1972. Science Press, 8 Brookstone Drive, Princeton, New Jersey 08540.

AMERICAN FACTORY DECOYS by Henry A. Fleckenstein Jr. Copyright 1981 by Henry A. Fleckenstein Jr. Schiffer Publishing Ltd., Box E, Exton, Pennsylvania 19341.

THE ART OF THE DECOY-AMERICAN BIRD CARVINGS by Adele Earnest. Published 1965 by Clarkson N. Potter. Crown, 419 Park Avenue South, New York, New York 10016.

AMERICAN SPORTING COLLECTORS HANDBOOK edited by Allan J. Liu. Copyright 1976 by the Winchester Press and published by Stoeger Publishing Company, 55 Ruta Court, South Hackensack, New Jersey 07606.

THE AMERICAN SPORTING COLLECTORS HANDBOOK, Revised Edition, edited by Allan J. Liu. Copyright 1982 by Allan J. Liu and published by the Winchester Press, 1421 South Sheridan Road, P. O. Box 1260, Tulsa, Oklahoma 74101.

THE BIRD DECOY by Paul A. Johnsgard. Copyright 1976. University of Nebraska Press.

CHESAPEAKE BAY DECOYS by R. H. Richardson. Copyright 1973. Crowhaven Publishers. OUT OF PRINT.

CHINCOTEAGUE CARVERS AND THEIR DECOYS by Barry and Velma Berkey. Copyright 1977. Tidewater Publishers, P. O. Box 109, Cambridge, Maryland 21613.

DECOYS OF THE ATLANTIC FLYWAY by George Ross Starr Jr. Copyright 1974. Winchester Press, 1421 South Sheridan Road, P. O. Box 1260, Tulsa, Oklahoma 74101.

DECOYS OF THE MID-ATLANTIC REGION by Henry A. Fleckenstein. Copyright 1979. Schiffer Publishing Ltd., Box E, Exton, Pennsylvania 19341.

DECOYS OF THE MISSISSIPPI FLYWAY by Alan G. Haid. Copyright 1981 by Alan G. Haid. Schiffer Publishing Ltd., Box E, Exton Pennsylvania 19341.

DECOYS AT THE SHELBURNE MUSEUM by William Kehoe and David Webster. Copyright 1961. Hobby House. Available from the Shelburne Museum, Shelburne, Vermont 05482.

DECOY COLLECTING PRIMER by Paul W. Casson. Copyright 1978 by Paul W. Casson. Paul S. Eriksson Publisher, Middlebury, Vermont.

DECOY COLLECTORS GUIDE by Harold D. Sorenson. Magazine reprints from 1963 through 1977. Available from the Ward Foundation, Battell Building, P. O. Box 703, Salisbury, Maryland 05753.

DECOYS OF THE SUSQUEHANNA FLATS AND THEIR MAKERS by J. Evans McKinney. Copyright 1978. Holly Press.

DECOYS AND DECOY CARVERS OF ILLINOIS by Forrest D. Loomis and Paul W. Parmalee. Copyright 1969. Northern Illinois University Press. Available from the Ward Foundation, P. O. Box 703, Salisbury, Maryland 21801.

FACTORY DECOYS OF MASON, STEVENS, DODGE AND PETERSON by John and Shirley Delph. Copyright 1980. Shiffer Publishing Ltd., Box E, Exton, Pennsylvania 19341.

GUNNING THE CHESAPEAKE by Roy Walsh. Copyright 1961. Tidewater Publishers, P. O. Box 109, Cambridge, Maryland 21613.

GUNNERS PARADISE; WILDFOWLING AND DECOYS ON LONG ISLAND by E. Jane Townsend. Available from the Ward Foundation, P. O. Box 703, Salisbury, Maryland 21801.

LOUISIANA DUCK DECOYS by Charles W. Frank, Jr. Copyright 1975 by Charles W. Frank, Jr. pelican Publishing Co., 630 Burmaster Street, Gretna, Louisiana 70053.

MARTHA'S VINEYARD DECOYS by Stanley Murphy. Copyright 1978. David R. Godine, Publisher, 306 Dartmouth Street, Boston, Massachusetts 02116.

MASON DECOYS by Byron Cheever. Copyright 1974. Hillcrest Publications, P. O. Box 246, Spanish Fork, Utah 84660.

NATIONAL DIRECTORY OF DECOY COLLECTORS by Gene and Linda Kangas, 6852 Ravenna Road, Painesville, Ohio 44077.

NEW ENGLAND DECOYS by John and Shirley Delph. Schiffer Publishing Lt., Box E, Exton, Pennsylvania 19341.

THE OUTLAW GUNNER by Harry Walsh. Copyright 1971. Tidewater Publishers, P. O. Box 109, Cambridge, Maryland 21613.

PIONEER DECOY CARVERS (a biography of the Ward brothers) by Barry, Velma and Richard Berkey. Copyright 1977. Tidewater Publishers, P. O. Box 109, Cambridge, Maryland 21613.

SHORE BIRD DECOYS by Henry A. Fleckenstein, Jr. Copyright 1980. Schiffer Publishing Ltd., Box E, Exton, Pennsylvania 19341.

SUSQUEHANNA RIVER DECOYS by Harold R. Buckwalter. Copyright 1978. Available from the Ward Foundation, P. O. Box 703, Salisbury, Maryland 21801.

L. T. WARD & BRO., WILDFOWL COUNTERFEITERS by Byron Cheever. Hillcrest Publications, P. O. Box 246, Spanish Fork, Utah 84660.

WILDFOWL DECOYS by Joel D. Barber. Copyright 1934 by Windward House and copyright 1954 by Dover Publications, Inc. Reissued by Dover in soft cover. Dover Publications, Inc., 180 Varick Street, New York, New York 10014.

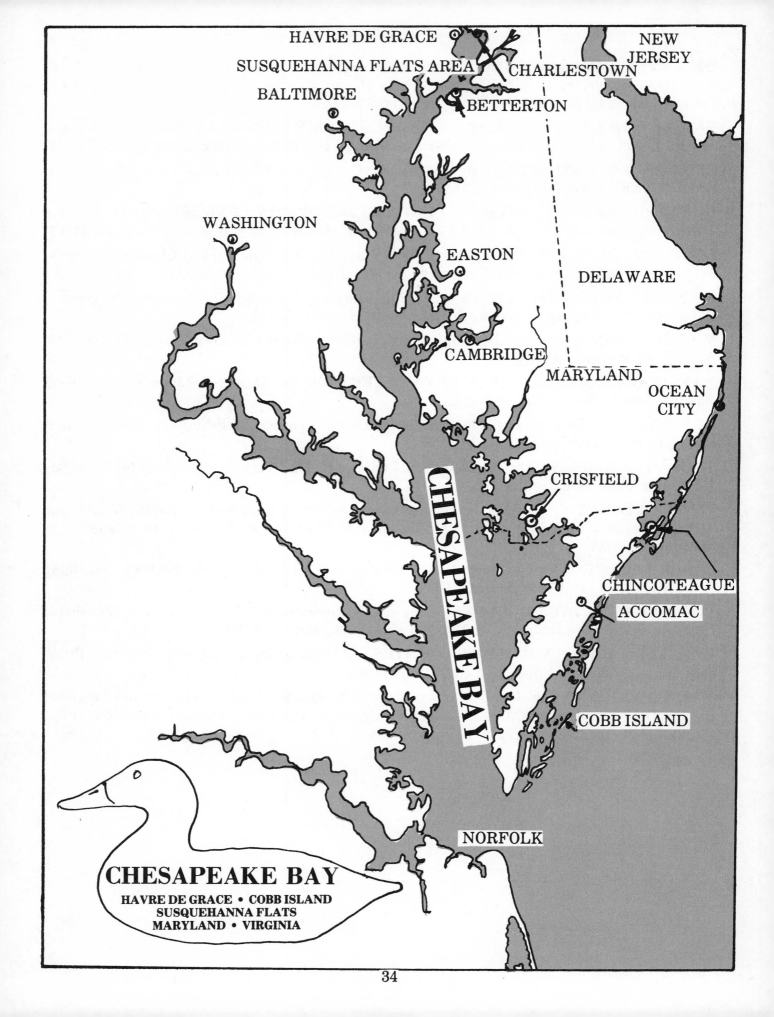

HAVRE DE GRACE

SUSQUEHANNA FLATS AREA

BALTIMORE

CHARLESTOWN

NEW JERSEY

BETTERTON

WASHINGTON

EASTON

DELAWARE

CAMBRIDGE

MARYLAND

OCEAN CITY

CHESAPEAKE BAY

CRISFIELD

CHINCOTEAGUE

ACCOMAC

COBB ISLAND

NORFOLK

CHESAPEAKE BAY

**HAVRE DE GRACE • COBB ISLAND
SUSQUEHANNA FLATS
MARYLAND • VIRGINIA**

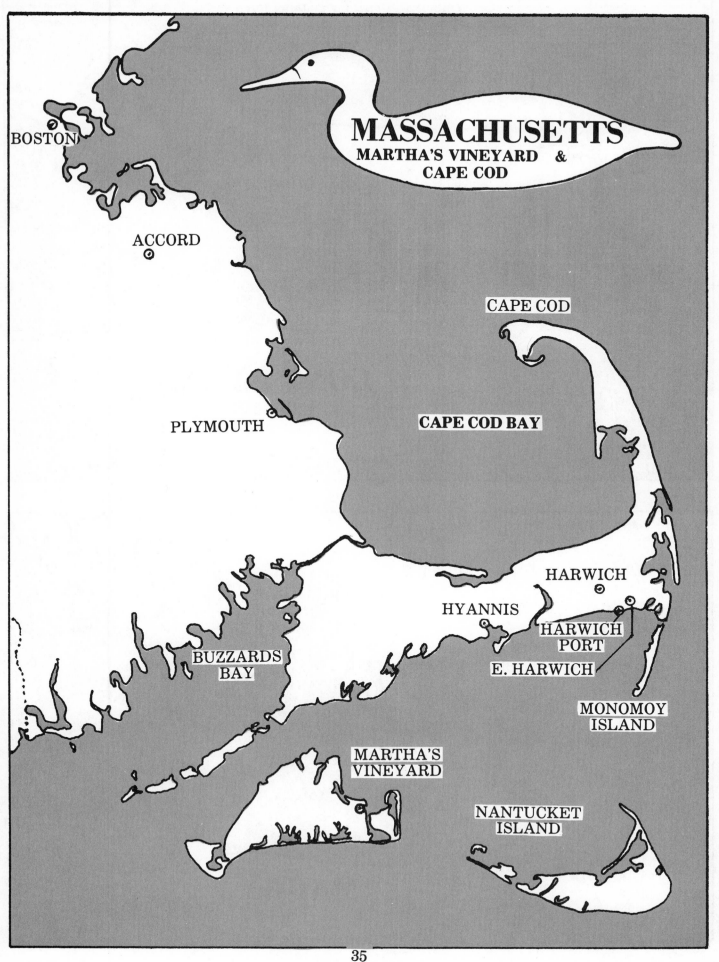

MASSACHUSETTS
MARTHA'S VINEYARD & CAPE COD

BOSTON

ACCORD

PLYMOUTH

CAPE COD

CAPE COD BAY

HARWICH

HYANNIS

HARWICH PORT

E. HARWICH

BUZZARDS BAY

MONOMOY ISLAND

MARTHA'S VINEYARD

NANTUCKET ISLAND

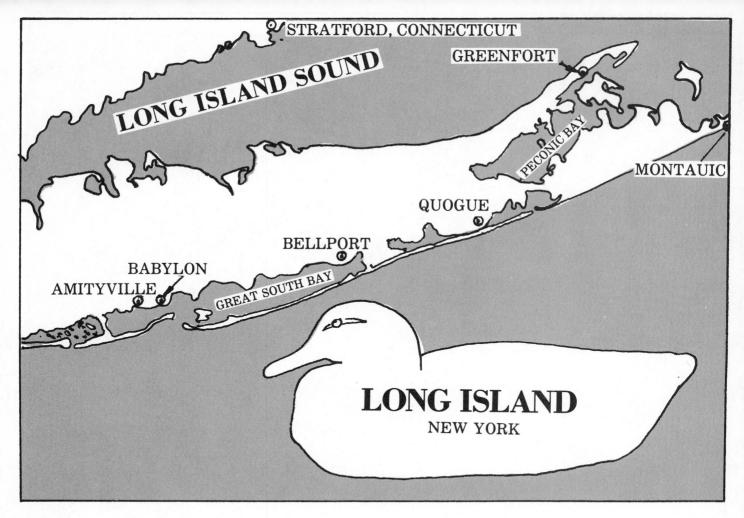

LONG ISLAND SOUND

STRATFORD, CONNECTICUT

GREENFORT

PECONIC BAY

MONTAUIC

QUOGUE

BELLPORT

BABYLON

AMITYVILLE

GREAT SOUTH BAY

LONG ISLAND
NEW YORK

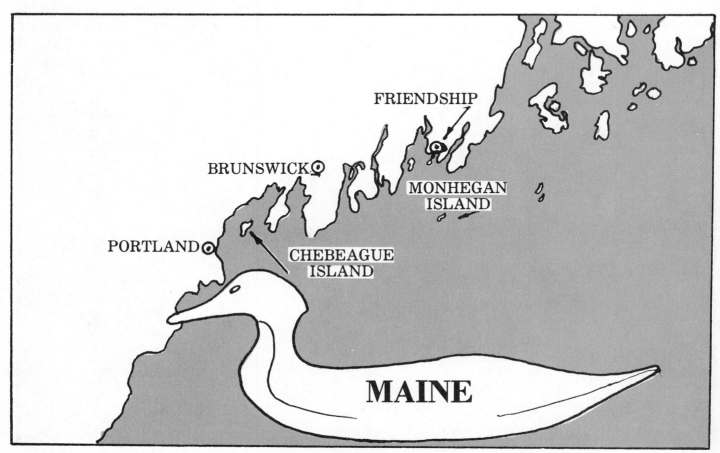

FRIENDSHIP

BRUNSWICK

MONHEGAN
ISLAND

PORTLAND

CHEBEAGUE
ISLAND

MAINE

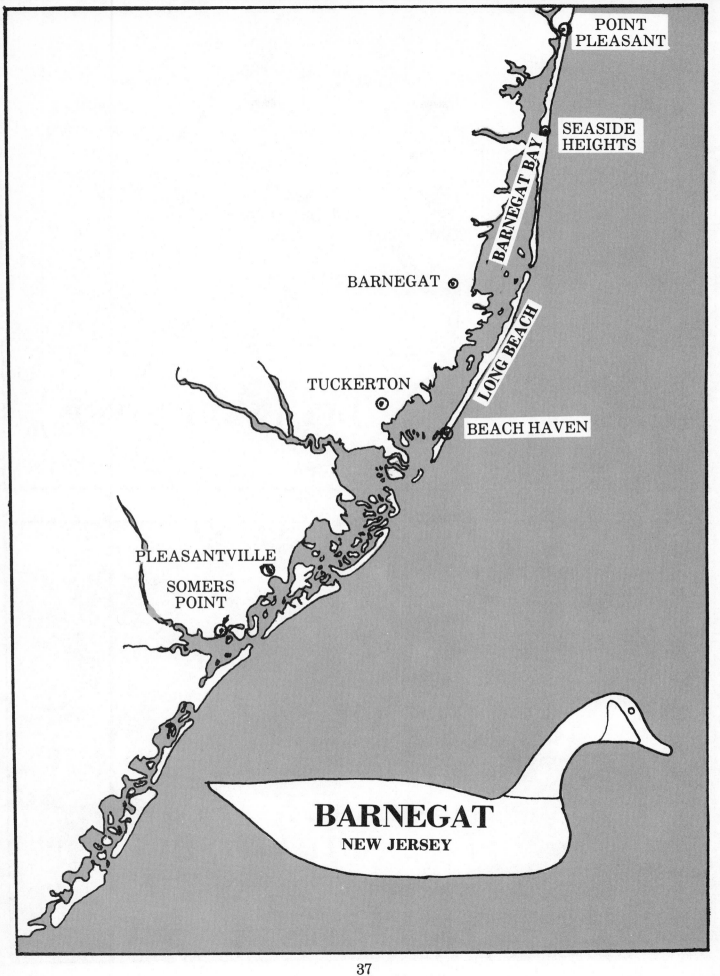

POINT
PLEASANT

SEASIDE
HEIGHTS

BARNEGAT BAY

BARNEGAT

LONG BEACH

TUCKERTON

BEACH HAVEN

PLEASANTVILLE

SOMERS
POINT

BARNEGAT
NEW JERSEY

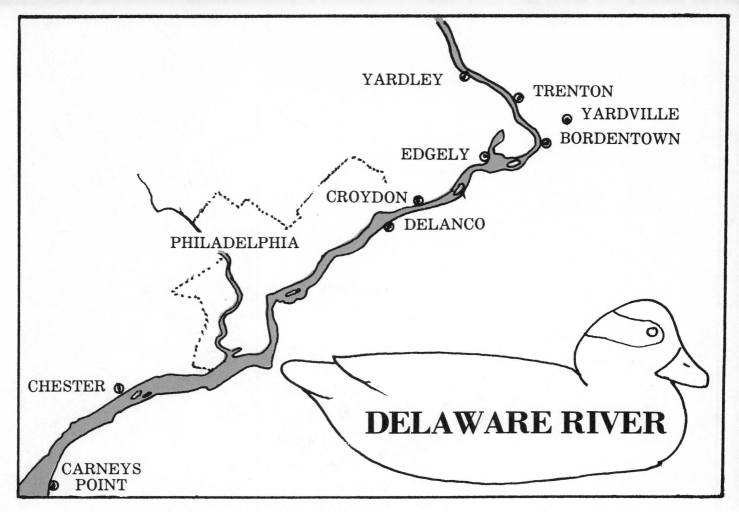

YARDLEY

TRENTON

YARDVILLE

BORDENTOWN

EDGELY

CROYDON

DELANCO

PHILADELPHIA

CHESTER

CARNEYS
POINT

DELAWARE RIVER

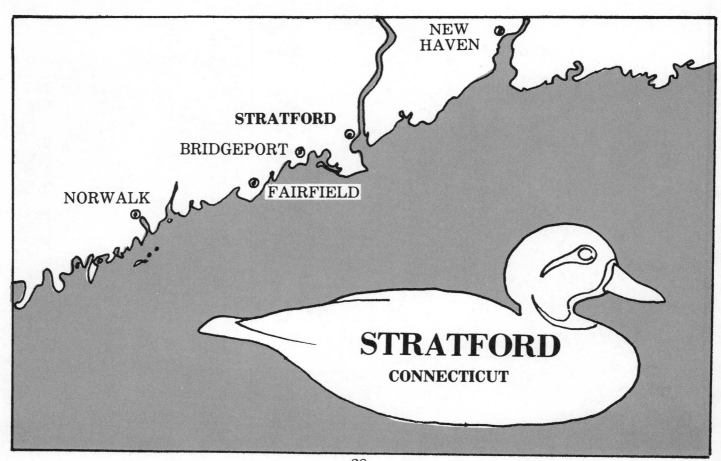

NEW
HAVEN

STRATFORD

BRIDGEPORT

NORWALK

FAIRFIELD

STRATFORD
CONNECTICUT

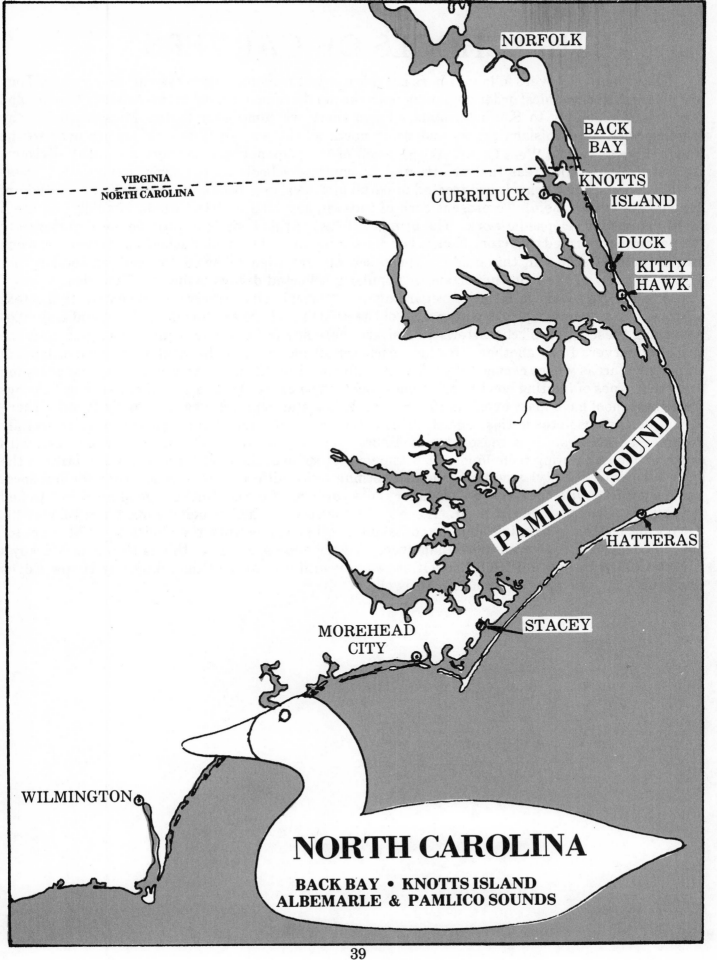

NORFOLK

BACK
BAY

VIRGINIA
NORTH CAROLINA

CURRITUCK

KNOTTS
ISLAND

DUCK

KITTY
HAWK

PAMLICO SOUND

HATTERAS

MOREHEAD
CITY

STACEY

WILMINGTON

NORTH CAROLINA

BACK BAY • KNOTTS ISLAND
ALBEMARLE & PAMLICO SOUNDS

THE SCHOOLS OF CARVERS

The schools of carvers following here are more or less regional within the various flyways. They are placed in geographical order beginning with the northernmost school in the Atlantic Flyway and proceeding southerly to South Carolina. From there we jump over to the Mississippi Flyway starting with the Louisiana School and going north all the way to Wisconsin thence over to the Pacific Flyway on the West Coast. Within each of the regional schools there are many divisions representing specific areas that are treated as separate schools by the serious collector. These smaller more specific schools are treated in detail in the various books that specialize in a study of the makers within them. To present each of these in any kind of detail would virtually require a multi-volume encyclopaedic work. The primary thrust of this book is to provide basic guidance to the new or uninformed collector. Hence, the consolidation of the smaller schools of carvers into one larger regional school in this guide. These schools are then followed by another section that discusses a few of the more important or popularly collected decoys made by "Factories".

A word of caution is in order regarding the "typical" characteristics presented in the text discussions and photo captions within each of the schools. There are few if any hard and fast rules governing these "typical" characteristics nor are there any definite line boundaries separating one school of carvers from another. Rather, each school blends into the next creating overlapping transitional areas where carvers of each were influenced by those of the other or by the changing areas and types of hunting conditions. Consequently you cannot treat a statement such as "Decoys from this school have glass eyes" as 100% true. It is a statement of what is **usually** found. There cannot be any absolutes in this regard. This is true even of some of the well-known and carefully documented makers. It is reasonable to assume that any maker might have experimented with construction or painting techniques. It is known that some of them who almost always utilized the same techniques or styles accomplished something quite different on special order for instance. Some were free with their carved heads for those carvers who could make a good body but lacked the ability to produce a decent head. There is also the case of a maker being a master at carving his decoys but lacking in painting ability and having another maker with the ability to paint them for him. The latter has occured more than once. A very good example of this is shown in Mackey's **American Bird Decoys** in PLATE 56. It shows a beautifully carved Scaup drake by Henry Keyes Chadwick that was painted by Elmer Crowell.

NOVA SCOTIA

The decoys typical of this school are represented by the drake and hen Eiders in the accompanying PLATES 19 and 20. The greatest majority of the makers of Nova Scotia made their decoys for hunting in the rough coastal waters of the area. Most of them are very sturdy and made by the two-piece solid body construction method. The head is attached directly to the body surface, not inletted or atop a shelf carved on the body as is common practice by makers farther south. When you examine the bottom of these decoys you will probably find evidence of their having been rigged "on a line", fore and aft. There may even be remnants of the leather thongs present at the front and rear of the decoy bottom. Use of leather thongs was the common method of providing line ties.

The painting of the decoys was not very elaborate because in the main they hunted sea ducks, not considered particularly wary. Hence, the simple, rather crude paint job.

Value Range for Nova Scotia Decoys .... $100 - 300

PLATE 19. A drake Eider from the Nova Scotia School. The maker of this decoy is not known. Two-piece solid body with the head turned slightly to the side.

PLATE 20. A hen Eider from the Nova Scotia School. The maker of this decoy is not known. Two-piece solid body with the head turned slightly to one side.

PLATE 21. A Scoter made by Sidney Butler of Halifax, Nova Scotia.

MAINE

The drake Red Breasted Merganser shown in PLATE 22 is about as representative of a decoy from the Maine School as you can ask for. It is somewhat oversize, constructed of solid wood with a flat bottom and has very slight, faintly visible raised wing carving. The head is inletted in a manner that is common to Maine decoys as well as is the carved oval eye representation. The overall look of Maine decoys is sleek and somewhat streamlined. Although most of the paint patterns the makers used were not quite so polished as that of the Merganser pictured in the photo they are in the same stylized type pattern for the most part.

Augustus Aaron "Gus" Wilson is one of the best known of makers from the Maine School. Common to all of his birds, save products of his later years, was the unusual carving of details on the underside of the lower mandible; an area of the head that few carvers ever paid much attention to as it would never be seen by a live bird being decoyed in. Other common characteristics of Wilson's decoys are the carved oval eyes, raised wing carving and carved details on both upper and lower mandibles.

Although Wilson wasn't the only one to carve decoys whose heads were ingeniously fashioned so that they would rock back and forth with wave action, if you were to find one of his rocking head Black Ducks you would have a real prize. From time to time he also carved decoys with mussels or fish in their bills, or with slots for insertion of a piece of leather or some such, simulating seaweed or fish.

Decoys from this school were generally made heavy and oversized to better fit the hunting conditions of the region. See map on page 36.

Value Range for Maine Decoys

George Huey .... $400 - 1000
Gus Wilson
    Mergansers and Black Ducks .... $500 - 3000
    Most others .... 500 - 1200
Other Makers from Maine .... 175 - 400

PLATE 22. A Red Breasted Merganser drake from the Maine School. The carving and construction details on this decoy are typical of the Maine decoys and are strikingly similar to that of Gus Wilson's products. It may be one of his but the paint pattern is more elaborate and polished than normally associated with his decoys.

PLATE 23. This male King Eider is placed in the Maine School because of its inletted head. As you can see it looks very much like a decoy from the Nova Scotia School. It could very well be from a transitional area between the schools but for the purposes of this book it is in the Maine School. Many collectors lump the two schools together.

MASSACHUSETTS

The Massachusetts School is where the first evidence of a widespread movement toward more refined decoys in that they are made in overall shape much more like a live bird. As a general rule however, they lack fine detailing such as wing carving or very intricate paint patterns, but they were well finished with fine sanding and the paint patterns more accurately reflect that of live birds than most earlier decoys.

An extraordinary exception to the above are the decoys of a maker from the Cape Cod area. Elmer Crowell of East Harwich, Massachusetts is acknowledged to be a master among makers from any school. The decoys he made from about 1900 to 1920 are those most sought by collectors. After that period his production of working decoys began to decline while his interest in the **art** of the decoy increased and he concentrated more and more on producing decorative or ornamental decoys. Crowell used a distinctive oval brand, but he did not initiate its use until about 1915. Some collectors consider his 1900 - 1915 unbranded decoys as being the most desirable. The brand is illustrated below in line drawing. It measures 3 - 1/8" x 1 - 7/8".

Later on, Crowell adopted a rectangular shaped brand. This later brand was also used by his son Cleon.

Elmer Crowell's decoys were made with solid white cedar bodies with heads carved from white pine as were all the typical Massachusetts School decoys. He was both an exceptional carver and painter. A common characteristic of his decoys is carved wings with the tips crossed. Additionally he used a rasp to simulate feathers on the breasts and the back of the heads. Almost all of his birds had glass eyes and the bottoms were wide and flat.

There are some decoys by Crowell that are atypical in style although his painting talent is obvious. These are from a rig he carved for the Monomoy Branting Club. They differ in construction in that they are so narrow-bodied and high that they had to be mounted on a triangular frame, usually in groups of three, to make them float upright.

As Crowell progressed his working decoys became less and less detailed insofar as carving details are concerned but, with one exception, his painting pattern remained as good as ever. This is illustrated by the fact that even when his birds lacked any wing carving at all, he still painted the wings beautifully and detailed to the point of his characteristic crossed wing tips. The exception is a group of Black Ducks he made for a sporting goods store. They are very plain with no carving detail on the body at all. The heads are characteristically rasped and the wing tips painted crossed. These decoys were stenciled on the bottom with the name of the store; "Iver Johnson".

In the photos accompanying this text is a Brant by Joe Lincoln from Accord, Massachusetts. This typical Lincoln decoy was made sometime before 1920. It has a carved separation between the bill and face, glass eyes and a one-piece solid cedar body.

The Canada Goose in the photo is also a Joe Lincoln decoy. The way this decoy is constructed is also common to Canada decoys of the school. The Slat-body is formed by bending lath-like narrow cedar slats over a frame. The earlier examples had canvas or similar material stretched over the body and then the finished product was painted. Later they dispensed with the practice of covering the wood with fabric and merely painted directly on the wood. The heads were carved from cedar normally.

The last carver illustrated as representative of this school is Henry Keyes Chadwick of Martha's Vineyard. It is estimated that he carved upwards of 2000 decoys during his decoy making years. His birds were also the typical one-piece solid cedar bodies with pine heads. They were flat-bottomed, beautifully carved decoys usually sporting glass eyes although he sometimes used both tack and painted eye representation. Usually there will be a hole evident on the bottom, beneath the head, through which he inserted a brass screw to hold it in position. His ballast weight was flush with the bottom or inletted. He would carve out a rounded hole in the bottom and pour in molten lead to accomplish this. See map on page 35.

Value Range for Massachusetts Decoys

Joe Lincoln . . . . $1000 - 2000*
Elmer Crowell . . . . 450 - 1500**
Henry Keyes Chadwick . . . . 200 - 800***

*Exceptional examples of Lincoln decoys have gone as high as $6000.
**Exceptional examples of Crowell decoys have gone as high as $1500 - 3000.
***Exceptional examples of Chadwick decoys have gone as high as $1200 - 1500.

PLATE 24. A Brant made by Joe Lincoln. Lincoln was a commercial decoy maker from Accord, Massachusetts. This Brant is beautifully formed and is a very typical Lincoln decoy with the one-piece solid body, glass eyes and a carved delineation between the bill and face.

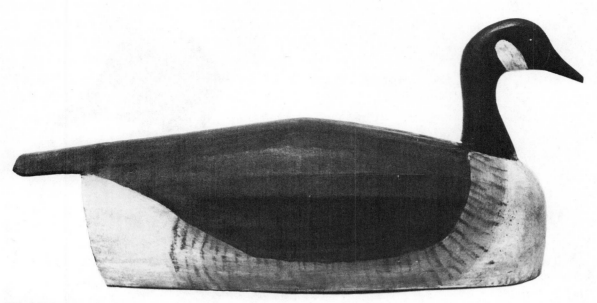

PLATE 25. Another decoy by Joe Lincoln. This is a slat-body Canada Goose. This particular decoy has a canvas cover indicating that it may be one of the earlier Massachusetts slat-body goose decoys (see text accompanying).

PLATE 26. Hen Goldeneye made by Henry Keyes Chadwick of Martha's Vineyard, Massachusetts. He made very strong and serviceable decoys that are quite typical of decoys of Martha's Vineyard makers. The flattened, turned down tail is characteristic. This decoy was made around 1925.

PLATE 27. This Chadwick Goldeneye drake is the mate to the hen Goldeneye in PLATE 26.

PLATE 28. This is one piece of a "double shadow" decoy attributed to Joe Lincoln. The "double shadow" usually consists of eight silhouettes of ducks, six of which nest between fixed decoys at either end. Sea Coots or Scoters.

CONNECTICUT (STRATFORD)

The Stratford area was home for three masters of decoy making: Albert Laing, Benjamin Holmes and Charles E. "Shang" Wheeler. These three represent the best of the makers in the area and their work is very representative of the typical styles and construction type normally used there. That these three men are the best of the school is a bit unusual in that none of them was a commercial maker. It is known that Shang Wheeler never sold any of his decoys and if either of the others did so it was probably a rare occurence. They made their decoys for themselves and friends and it is not very likely that any one of them carved more than a few hundred in their lifetime. This fairly low production probably accounts for the superb workmanship exhibited in their respective decoys.

Common to all three of them is the exaggerated upswept breasts carved to enable the decoys to float in and over ice and slush frequently encountered in the waters of the area. In addition each of them utilized a two-piece hollow body with a depression carved in the body top just behind the head. The latter is sometimes referred to as a "neck notch".

Even with these common characteristics they are fairly easily distinguished from each other. When Laing carved his birds he almost invariably carved his last name quite clearly in large letters on the bottom. Even if this brand is not present you can tell his from Holmes birds because Laing always made his two-piece bodies in more or less equal upper and lower halves with the joint being above the waterline. Holmes used a half inch bottom board to close up the bottom of the hollowed out body. The best way to distinguish Wheeler decoys from the others is by being familiar with his highly sophisticated painting style.

The majority of decoys from the Stratford area are hollow constructed with glass eyes, the exaggerated breasts, and beautiful paint jobs often using the comb-feather technique. When bottom boards were used they will generally be of a 1/2" to 5/8" thickness. When the original weight is present it will usually be what is referred to as the Connecticut "Pear-shaped Weight". This weight, really more like a teardrop cut in half, was attached with a brass screw so that the hunter could loosen the screw allowing him to adjust the weight for balancing the floating decoy. The species most often found is the Black Duck as it was the species hunted most often.

The Pintail in the accompanying photos was made by Shang Wheeler about 1925. This decoy has its original paint and is a superb example of Wheeler's talent as a maker. Also you will find another photo of the same decoy. You will note in that photo that Wheeler took the extra trouble to apply his painting talent even to the bottom of the decoy. This is common to all of his decoys of puddle duck species.

The example of Ben Holmes decoys illustrated in the accompanying photos is like most decoys of the school that were made with bottom boards.

The Bliss Black Duck illustrated in bottom view presents the overall pear shape characteristic of decoys of the area.

As a general rule decoys of the school are of the two-piece hollow body variety. Early makers used glass eyes later evolving to painted eyes. They did not often use tack eyes apparently. See map on page 38.

Value Range for Stratford Decoys

Ben Holmes . . . . $500 - 1500
Charles "Shang" Wheeler . . . . 750 - 1800*
Roswell Bliss . . . . 250 - 650

*Some exceptional Wheeler decoys have gone in excess of $3500.

PLATE 29. A Pintail by Charles ("Shang") Wheeler made about 1932. This excellent decoy has its original paint in quite good condition, glass eyes, detail carving of mandibles, nares and differential carving betwen the face and bill. The body is comb-feather painted and the tail is fashioned from a piece or sheet copper.

PLATE 30. Bottom view of the same Wheeler Pintail shown above. Note the unusual comb-feather detail painting on the bottom. Few makers of any school took the extra trouble to paint the bottom of their decoys with any design at all. This is a characteristic found on all of Wheeler's puddle duck species. The ballast weight is the classic Connecticut (Stratford) adjustable pear shaped or "Teardrop" weight.

PLATE 31. A Scaup drake made by Benjamin Holmes. This decoy has glass eyes, comb-feather painting, the very typical paddle-like tail and the protruding upswept breast of the Stratford decoys.

PLATE 32. This Black Duck by Roswell Bliss serves to illustrate more common characteristics of the Stratford School; paddle tail, protruding breast and the groove behind the head.

PLATE 33. Bottom view of the Bliss Black Duck in PLATE 32. Bliss used the bottom-board construction technique. Note the brand stating that the decoy was built by Bliss for Ken Peck in 1912. The Bliss brand is found on most of his pre-1940 decoys. You can also see the head-holding dowell on the bottom just aft of the anchor line tie.

NEW YORK STATE

The New York State School boasted very few commercial carvers, but one who did make his living as a maker of decoys was Frank Lewis of Ogdensburg. He carved commercially for about ten years and his output was literally in the thousands. He himself is known to have stated that in one particular year alone he carved over a thousand. His birds and those of Sam Denny are good examples of the decoys from the school, however styles did vary widely within the area.

Frank Lewis carved Broadbills, Redheads and Whistlers all utilizing the same body and head differentiating the species with paint patterns only. The head/neck was inletted into a body with a very pronounced hump in the back. This unique characteristic gave rise to a descriptive term used by collectors: "Ogdensburg Humpbacks".

Lewis decoys are not difficult to identify once you have seen one, but to master identification of most makers from the New York State School will probably prove to be the most difficult of all. It seems like everybody and his brother was into making decoys and their products vary quite a bit.

The other fairly good representative maker in the school is Sam Denny from the St. Lawrence River area. Two of his decoys are illustrated in PLATES 35 & 36. His decoys typically have exaggerated, protruding breasts similar to those of the Stratford decoys but differ somewhat in that they have a sharp chine, the front of the breast is flattened considerably and almost pointed at the top. Denny did not use inletted heads but rather attached them to a shelf carved onto the body with a screw. $50 - 250.

Value Ranges for New York State Decoys

Sam Denny	$50 - 250
Frank Coombs	125 - 350
Ken Anger (See Plate 40)	250 - 500
Frank Lewis	50 - 200
Chaucy Wheeler	200 - 550

PLATE 34. Frank Lewis of Ogdensburg, New York made this hen Scaup. Note the carved concave head sides. This is typical of his decoys. The bird is simply but effectively carved and painted. It has an inletted head/neck.

PLATE 35. An exceptionally graceful Sam Denny Black Duck from St. Lawrence River/Alexandria Bay area of New York State. Note the definite shelf carved to receive the head and the flattened protruding breast. The head is attached from the bottom through a recessed hole that is plugged with a cork to protect it. All characteristics typical of Denny decoys.

PLATE 36. Another New York School bird. Frank Coombs of the Alexandria Bay area made this hen Bluebill. It has a solid body, glass eyes and original paint. Ca. 1925.

PLATE 37. This solid body Black Duck decoy was made by Ken Anger of Dunnville, Ontario, Canada. Dunnville is located on the far northeastern shore of Lake Erie. It is quite close to Buffalo, New York, but Anger's style seems more like those of the Michigan School. Nevertheless, William Mackey in his book **American Bird Decoys**, places Anger in the New York School. His mastery of the rasp in imparting a beautiful feather texture to his decoys earned him the nickname, "The Raspmaster". (New York State School)

PLATE 38. Another decoy made by Sam Denny. This Goldeneye drake exhibits the same characteristics as the Black Duck in Plate 35. It is a better example of the typical straight-line flattened breast on his decoys.

LONG ISLAND

The greatest number of decoys from the Long Island School are constructed of solid wood but there are a few hollow body decoys to be found. This school is where root heads and cork body birds first gained widespread popularity among makers of the Atlantic Coast. The root heads are most often found on Mergansers, Pheasants, Brants and Black Ducks. The cork body decoys are usually found made in two or more layers atop a pine bottom board.

Some general observations about wooden Long Island birds are that they are usually of solid construction with a carved shelf for the mounting of the head and there is no detail carving on the face or bill. Carved eye representation, however, is very common. They sometimes used tack eyes. The decoys are simply constructed with no wing or feather carving. They are well sanded and simply but nicely finished in paint patterns.

A common ballast weight for Long Island decoys is a lead weight that has been cast in sand or the hollow in a tree limb or piece of driftwood.

The two Brants and the Black Duck in the accompanying illustrations are fairly typical of decoys from this school.

Heron, Wood Duck and Old Squaw decoys from the Long Island school are particularly rare in that order of precedence. They range in value from $750 to as high as $3000. Good Mergansers can be valued up to about $500 and other species of decoys from the school range upwards from around $75 with most topping out at about $200. See map on page 36.

PLATE 39. This early 20th Century Black Duck decoy was made by a well known market hunting family from Long Island. Typically they refined their decoys to the degree shown in the photo. The head is not made from a root but rather nicely carved from a block of wood and attached to the typical shelf carving though this shelf is only slightly discernable. The body is of solid wood with a flat bottom and a back groove common to Verity family decoys. The eyes are carved and their bills and faces lack any carving details. It is known that the family did do a bit of wing carving from time to time.

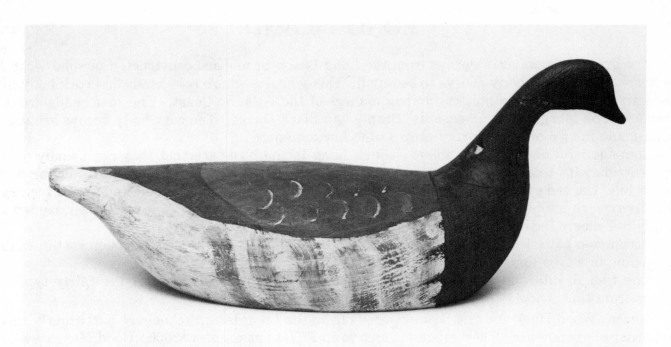

PLATE 40. This is another Long Island School Brant. As in the case of the other Brant the carver of this one is not known. What is known is that it came from Bellport and is about 100 years old. It has the typical shelf carving and a holly root head with brass tack eyes.

PLATE 41. A very fine Long Island Brant decoy with original paint. The maker of this decoy is not known but was obviously talented. This bird sports the typical root head found on Long Island decoys but only a slight hint of the shelf for the neck/head attachment can be detected. It has carved eye representation but no face or bill carving details.

PLATE 42. This photo shows the bottom of the Brant in PLATE 41. The brand "Suydam" is quite significant in that it belonged to a very prominant Long Island family. They apparently were choosey about the decoys they hunted over for their brand shows up on many excellent decoys from the region. Another significant feature on the bottom is the presence of holes in a pattern that indicates that the decoy was used as a wing decoy. A wooden wing decoy is a rare bird indeed.

BARNEGAT BAY (NEW JERSEY)

Just about all the makers of the Barnegat Bay area in New Jersey fashioned their decoys from white cedar using the two-piece hollow body method. The heads were carved from white cedar as well. It is exceedingly unusual to find a solid body decoy from this school. Makers from the Barnegat School were masters of the two-piece hollow body style. The bodies they made are proportionally smaller than those from most of the other schools on the Atlantic Coast and the heads were slightly out of scale, being somewhat large for the bodies. The heads were attached to the body on a carved shelf. The two pieces hollowed out to make the body were joined at a seam above the waterline. The decoys were very light and for ballast the makers used pads cut from sheet lead. Most of the time these lead pad weights were attached to the bottom only after the decoy had been painted. Not all makers adhered to this practice and one notable exception was a maker named Harry V. Shourds. Shourds ballasted his decoys by carving out a rectangular hole in the bottom and pouring molten lead into it (see PLATE 46). He painted the decoy **after** this operation.

There were other makers in the area that used this method of ballasting but Shourds is the best known to them. See map on page 37.

Value Ranges for Barnegat Decoys

Harry V. Shourds	$500 - 1200
Ellis Parker	100 - 500
Jesse Birdsall	100 - 350
Lloyd Johnson	200 - 400

PLATE 43. A Brant made by Ellis Parker of Beach Haven in New Jersey. This is a classic example of white cedar two-piece hollow-body New Jersey Decoy. The joint of the two halves is above the waterline, has a leather thong for anchor line attachment. If you look closely, you may be able to discern the woodscrew eye. This is not usual. Parker apparently ran out of glass eyes and used the screws to save time. It is interesting to note the screw slots are oriented horizontally as if the bird were sleeping.

PLATE 44. This Barnegat School Black Duck decoy was made by Jesse Birdsall. Note the definite shelf carving. It has the typical lead pad weight. You may not be able to see it but there is a faint hint of wing carving detail on this particular decoy.

PLATE 45. Black Duck by Harry V. Shourds of Tuckerton, New Jersey. This is another classic example of a New Jersey decoy with shelf, carved bill and fine details, tack eyes, and the tail extending more or less from the center of the body. This latter is characteristic of most New Jersey decoys excepting Brants and Geese.

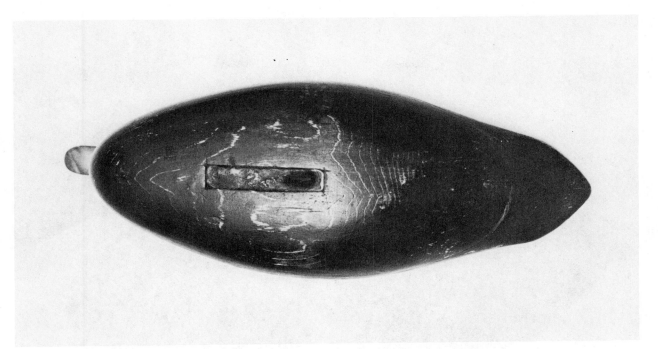

PLATE 46. This photo is of the bottom of the above Shourds Black Duck. It shows the exterior view of the inletted lead weight discussed in the accompanying text. If you were to take an X-ray of the bird, you could see that Shourds carved down and then horizontally a bit so that when the lead was poured in it turned about 90°. This held the weight in the body very effectively, if it were to become loose as a result of the wood expanding or contracting.

PLATE 47. Widgeon Drake by Lloyd Johnson. This New Jersey decoy has pronounced flat bottom, glass eyes and excellent original paint. It has a lead pad weight that was placed on the decoy after the paint job was applied.

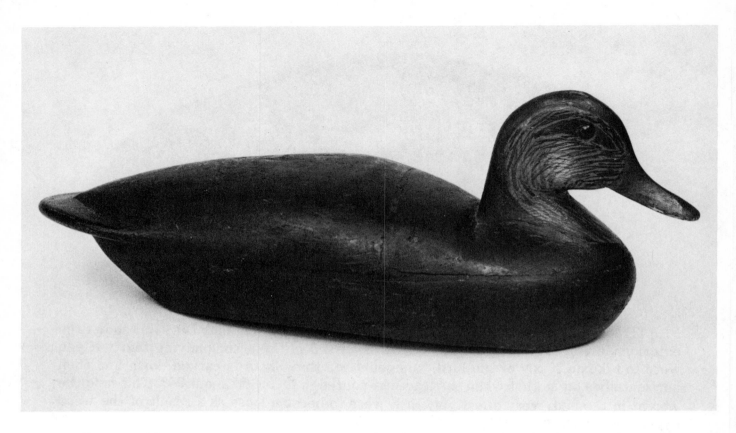

PLATE 48. Black Duck made by Walter Bush of Newark, New Jersey. Notice the unusual construction of this hollow body decoy. The upper one-half is made in two sections, the forward section being part of the head and neck.

PLATE 49. This New Jersey School Merganser was made by Chip Alsop. It has a two-piece hollow body, tack eyes, a neck notch and a rectangular inletted ballast weight.

PLATE 50. A Scaup drake decoy by New Jersey School maker Dipper Ortley. Ortley, from Point Pleasant, N. J.,   used painted eyes and the two-piece hollow body construction typical of this school This is a fairly late decoy, having been made in the 1950's.

PLATE 51. This swimming Mallard drake is attributed to J. Eugene Hendrickson. This New Jersey maker's decoys are made in the traditional fine hollow-body New Jersey style. His tails usually end in something of a point, as is the one in the photograph here. Glass eyes and detailed bill, face carving and, often, comb feather painting characterize his birds. He frequently branded his birds with his initials "JEH".

DELAWARE RIVER

Decoys of the Delaware River School have hardly any rivals in other school as a group when it comes to the beauty of carving and painting. As a whole the decoys made by the carvers of this school are considered by many, many collectors to be the most desirable from most aspects of collecting.

The method of hunting practiced in the area dictated that the decoys hunted over be made as much like the real thing as was possible. The typical hunter in the area used a sculling boat to almost bushwack the ducks. The hunter would set out his rig of decoys at known or likely feeding grounds, pull back upstream as much as three quarters of a mile and wait for the ducks to pitch in and land. He then would very carefully and silently scull down to within killing range and fire away. Because of this method the Delaware River decoy not only had to be good enough to decoy the birds down, but to still fool them once they had landed among them. The latter requirement was to give the waiting hunter time to scull back down to his prey.

The decoys had to be extremely realistic in both carving conformation and paint pattern. Most of them have heads squat down on the body with little or no neck showing at all. This conveyed an attitude of content ducks who sense no danger, to the live ones above.

The decoys are full breasted and constructed in the two-piece hollow manner; few bottom board types were made. Heads are mounted directly to the body in the low head or sleeping position. They usually had glass eyes although the other types have been found. A very significant characteristic common to them is extremely well-carved tails and wings.

As a rule the paint patterns were extraordinarily realistic and often quite intricate.

As you go down stream on the river you find that the makers paid less and less attention to the carving of wings and tails, but they did continue to pay close attention to the need for painting their decoys in the same realistic and characteristic pattern style.

The John Dawson and John English decoys pictured in the accompanying plates serve well to illustrate the style which is that of Delaware River School of carvers. See map on page 38.

Value Ranges for Delaware River Decoys

John Dawson	$400 - 200
John English	250 - 750
John McLaughlin	350 - 1000

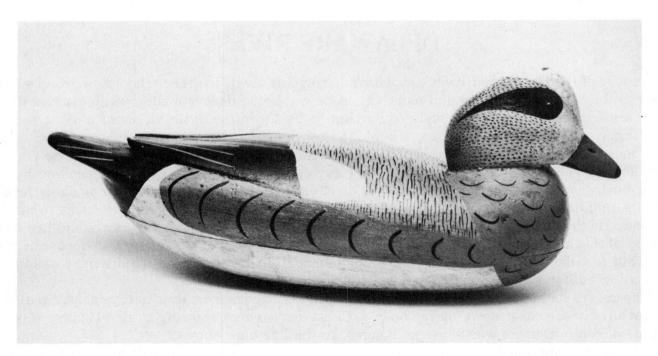

PLATE 52. A Widgeon drake made by John Dawson of Trenton and Duck Island in New Jersey. This decoy exhibits the classic squat position of the head so common to the Delaware School as well as the typical delicately sculpted wings and tail.

PLATE 53. John English, Florence, New Jersey, made this Black Duck. This bird shows just a hint of neck, but still the overall appearance conveys the necessary restful, contentment. The photograph doesn't do justice to the subtle beauty of the paint pattern.

PLATE 54. This Canada Goose decoy was made by M. L. Perkins of Delano, New Jersey. Delano is on the Delaware River and Perkins is part of the Delaware River School of makers. This Canada Goose has glass eyes, raised wing carving, and the body is of three-piece hollow construction. Head and face have nice carving details.

PLATE 55. William Quinn of Yardley, Pennsylvania, made this superb Delaware River School Black Duck sleeper. It is a hollow body decoy with glass eyes, raised wing carving, and a carved tail typical of his birds.

PLATE 56. Drake Mallard. Delaware River low head. Two-piece hollow body; glass
eyes; beautifully carved tail, wings; raised feather pattern on body; face and bill detail;
lead pad weight; leather thong anchor line ties.

PLATE 57. Hen Mallard mate to the drake Mallard in PLATE 56.

SUSQUEHANNA FLATS

Of all the areas of the Chesapeake Bay, the Susquehanna Flats could be considered the one where market gunners and their sink boxes reigned supreme before the 1918 migratory bird legislation. These market hunters often used several hundred decoys in their rigs, consequently there were literally thousands of decoys made in the region. The huge numbers made, notwithstanding, are not evidenced by huge numbers surviving today, although there are still many found.

The types of decoys made in the Susquehanna Flats school share similar basic construction techniques and decoy style, and the difference between these decoys and those used in other schools of the Chesapeake can also be told by observing the species of wildfowl hunted. For example, the majority of decoys from the Susquehanna Flats are Canvasbacks, Redheads and Broadbills and farther down the Bay the primary targets were puddle ducks such as Teal and Mallards. Keep in mind the enormous size of the bay; there can be a 300 mile separation between schools of carvers on the Chesapeake.

The decoys of the Flats area are generally solid pine or cedar bodied with shelf carving for attaching the head/neck. One exception to this is found on decoys by some makers from Havre de Grace. **Earliest** decoys had very good carving delineation between the face and bill, carved mandibles and necks, and forged iron keels or ballast weights. Later, when lead became more readily available, the weights were cast by pouring the molten lead into depressions in sand (sand cast) or natural or gouged out depressions in wood. Less attention was paid to detail face and bill carving, but the overall conformation remained relatively unchanged. Just about all decoys from this school have round bottoms and are broad-breasted. Many of them are found with a slight ridge down the back.

Anchor line ties on earlier Flats decoys are usually of the leather thong type, but after around 1900-1920 the ring and staple type came into and remained in constant use all over the Chesapeake Bay.

John "Daddy" Holly of Havre de Grace, Maryland, is one of the most famous makers associated with the Susquehanna Flats. See map on page 34.

Value Ranges for Susquehanna Flats Decoys

John "Daddy" Holly .... $200 - 750
Ben Dye .... 150 - 500
R. Madison Mitchell .... 100 - 400

PLATE 58. A very early Susquehanna Flats Drake Canvasback decoy made by Ben Dye of Havre de Grace, Maryland. This decoy is about as good an example of early Flats decoys as you could ask for. It has the forged iron keel driven into the bottom (sometimes called a "horseshoe keel"); a solid color rounded bottom body; eyes impressed (Dye and many other early makers used a 32 calibre shell casing to impress the eyes into the wood); and fine carving details on the face and bill.

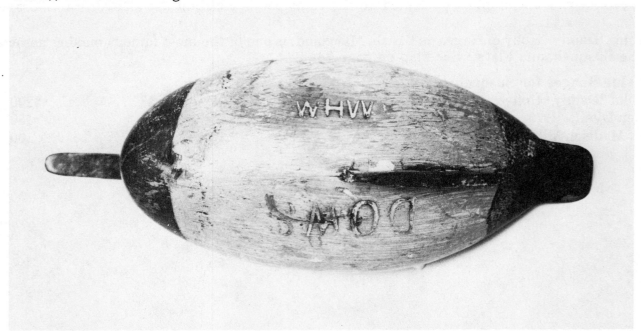

PLATE 59. Bottom view of the Ben Dye Canvasback in Plate 58. This shows user brands "WHW" and "DOWS" and the forged iron keel driven into the bottom. "DOWS" was Thomas Dows and "WHW" was his grandson, Watson Henry Webb. This type of provenance is valuable in determining vintage.

74

PLATE 60. A hen Canvasback made by Susquehanna Flats maker Charles Barnard. A **hen** Canvasback is difficult to locate generally. This is one of a pair of Barnard Canvasbacks (see Plate 61). It illustrates the common Flats decoy characteristics and conformation and serves well to illustrate the cast lead weight discussed in the accompanying text.

PLATE 61. The drake Canvasback, mate to the above Charles Bernard hen Canvas back. Matched pairs such as this are difficult to obtain as hens are seldom found.

PLATE 62. A very old hen Canvasback by John B. Graham of Charlestown, Maryland. This is quite typical of Graham's Canvasbacks. Note the cast lead weight. This is the original weight and is one of the earliest examples of cast lead weighted decoys from the Susquehanna Flats.

PLATE 63. A bottom view of the Graham Canvasback in the preceding plate. Excellent view of his typical lead weight. The ring and staple anchor line tie common to many Susquehanna Flats decoys is evident in this photo. The "P. K. Barnes" brand is found on many good early Flats decoys.

PLATE 64. A drake Canvasback by Scott Jackson that illustrates a little different style than the ordinary Susquehanna Flats decoy. It has a long upward swept tail not common in decoys from this school nor is it characteristic of Canvasback ducks. Just about all Jackson's decoys have this slightly upswept tail.

PLATE 65. R. Madison Mitchell made this Canvasback drake from the Susquehanna Flats. He made decoys from the 1930's up to around 1960 and collectors will likely encounter one of his decoys, if seeking decoys from the Chesapeake Bay area. He was an undertaker in Havre de Grace, Maryland, and probably made more wooden decoys than any other maker in Maryland. The ring and staple anchor line tie was just about always used by Mitchell. He made all his canvasbacks just like the one in this photo.

PLATE 66. A Charlie "Speed" Joiner drake Canvasback. Joiner was from Betterton, Maryland, on the Susquehanna Flats. This decoy has ring and staple anchor line tie and typical shape cast ballast weight.

PLATE 67. This is a folding two-dimensional Canvasback shadow decoy rig. Said to have come from the Chesapeake Bay area. Unsubstantiated.

PLATE 68. "Daddy" Holley drake Scaup. From Havre de Grace, Maryland, "Daddy" Holley's decoys are from the Susquehanna Flats School. Note the iron keel driven into the bottom of the decoy.

PLATE 69. A solid body, painted eye decoy from the Susquehanna Flats. Made by Paul Gibson of Havre de Grace, Maryland.

PLATE 70. Canvasback hen by R. Madison Mitchell from Havre de Grace, Maryland. Painted eyes and ballast weight typical of his decoys. From the Susquehanna Flats School.

PLATE 71. Pre-1900 Canvasback drake from Chesapeake Bay made by Henry Lockhard from Elk Neck, Maryland. Ring and staple. May have had tack or glass eyes at one time — now painted. Susquehanna Flats School.

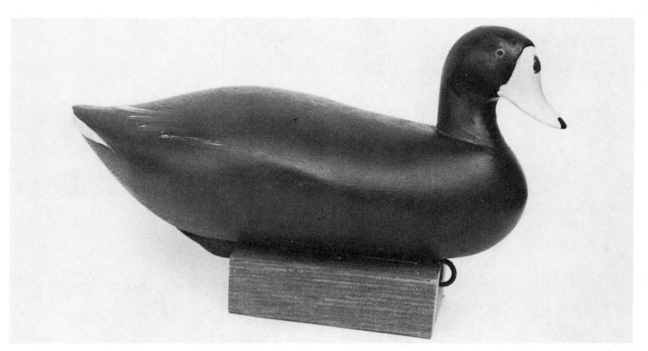

PLATE 72. A Scoter by R. Madison Mitchell from Havre de Grace, Maryland. Painted eyes, ballast weight and ring and staple anchor line tie typical of this oversize Susquehanna Flats, Mitchell decoy.

PLATE 73. A nice Susquehanna Flats Canvasback decoy by Robert S. Sellers. This maker is still hunting in the Flats and uses the old scull boat method of hunting.

PLATE 74. A Susquehanna Flats decoy made by Walter D. Sellers. Sellers, now deceased, was the brother of the above Robert S. Sellers.

MARYLAND EASTERN SHORE
(DORCHESTER COUNTY)

Although this is not really considered a true school of makers, there was a commercial decoy maker of note from Cambridge, Maryland, whose birds are well worth pursuit. Ed Phillips sold most of his decoys to hometown people and for a few gunning rigs. His decoys haven't achieved the prominence of some other decoys of the Chesapeake Bay area because he didn't produce them in nearly the numbers some of the other good carvers of the region produced. They are, however, excellent decoys. The decoys are not quite so rounded bottom as others of the region but are semi-rounded (not completely rounded nor completely flat-bottomed). The bodies are quite graceful and necks usually exhibit a backward arch. Almost all have carved eye representation, very well made and painted. Phillips frequently used the scratch feather painting technique.

All Phillips decoys have a sheet lead ballast weight on the bottom and an anchor line tie made of sheet copper bent into a loop and attached with a copper nail, if the original is present.

The bodies are solid as is characteristic of Chesapeake Bay area decoys. The necks are attached by a dowel rod. He made Canvasbacks, Pintails, Widgeon, Black Ducks, Redheads, and Canada Geese. See map on page 34.

Value Ranges for Maryland Eastern Shore Decoys

Ed Phillips . . . . $100 - 350

PLATE 75. An Ed Phillips drake Pintail decoy. A solid body decoy with carved eyes and scratch feather painting. This decoy illustrates the semi-round bottom discussed in the accompanying text. A beautifully carved and painted decoy by this Cambridge, Maryland, commercial decoy maker.

PLATE 76. This Canada Goose is also by Ed Phillips. If you look closely at the back of the head you can see the neck-attaching dowel rod protruding slightly. This long dowel is typical of the way Phillips attached his head/necks.

CRISFIELD (MARYLAND)

Just about all decoys from his school of carvers exhibit the same construction details. They are solid body decoys typical of the Chesapeake Bay birds, but here is where the first appearance of the true flat-bottom decoys occurs in the bay. Typically Crisfield decoys are slightly oversize, narrow breasted, wide in the hip area, and flat-bottomed with a high tail usually coming out of the top of the body as opposed to below, toward or at the middle of the rear end. The decoys were weighted with just about anything that might be handy to the maker at the time, so it is not a reliable characteristic.

The beginnings of the fine decoys of the Crisfield School are thought to be found in the Sterling family and perhaps Elwood Dye products. The most famous carvers of the school are Lemuel T. Ward, Sr. and his sons, Lem. Jr. and Steve. It was the Wards who took the carving and painting techniques the early Crisfield makers developed and refined them to a high art. The Ward Brothers were by and large the most prolific decoy makers in the Chesapeake Bay area. They are recognized today as those most deserving of note of all the Maryland makers. The painting techniques they developed and used on **working** decoys were as good as much of the delicate work found on today's contemporary carvings. Their decoys were painted so beautifully that many were bought not for hunting over but to use as decoration.

The photos in Plate 78 through Plate 82 serve very nicely to illustrate the progression of refinement in Crisfield School decoys from the earliest days to the Wards' latest working decoys.

Value Ranges for Crisfield Decoys

Ward Brothers . . . . $300 - 1600
Sterling Family . . . . 300 - 1200

Decoys from both of these groups have brought far in excess of these figures from time to time but the ranges above are the norm for an average shape working decoy. See map on page 34.

PLATE 77. This c. 1900 Canada Goose is a very early Crisfield decoy attributed to the Sterling family. Exhibits characteristics common to the school, i.e., the narrow breast, wide hips and flat bottom.

PLATE 78. Hen Goldeneye by Noah Sterling made around 1915.

PLATE 79. This Canada Goose decoy was made about 1920 by L. Travis Ward Sr. It is a fine example in original paint. Shows the beginning of the refinement in construction and paint techniques begun by the Wards. Excellent example of scratch feather pattern painting technique.

PLATE 80. A Ward Brothers balsa body Pintail drake. Keeled with the weights attached.

PLATE 81. Drake Pintail carved by Steve Ward Jr. and painted by Steve Ward Jr. Made of balsa wood. Although this one has no eyes, that is not significant. They occur with no eyes, painted eyes and glass eyes. This particular decoy and the following mate in Plate 82 are both from the Ward Brothers' personal hunting rig.

PLATE 82. Hen Pintail by the Ward Brothers. A match to the Drake Pintail in Plate 81.

PLATE 83. A Ward Brothers Canvasback Drake in original paint. This decoy is solid cedar, has glass eyes and is a classic 1936 model Ward Brothers Canvasback. Collectors call these decoys "Classic '36's".

A Mallard drake
by South Carolina maker
Hucks Cains.

This hen Mallard was made by
Hucks Cains of South Carolina.

A drake Mallard from South
Carolina. This particular decoy
illustrates what is known as the
"raised wing" model by collectors of
South Carolina decoys attributed to
the Cains brothers.

This is a typical Barnegat Bay area calling Wood Duck drake. The maker of this two piece hollow white cedar decoy is not known.

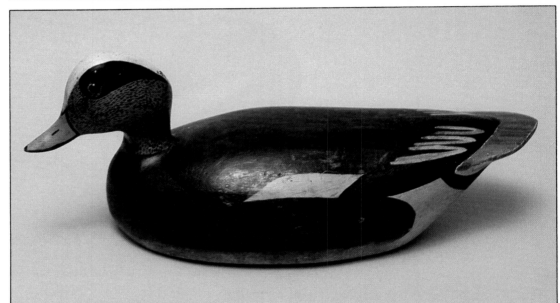

Widgeon drake by Lloyd Johnson. This New Jersey decoy has a flat bottom and glass eyes.

Drake Widgeon made by Miles Hancock of Chincoteague, Virginia

This sleeper Wood Duck drake is from the Barnegat Bay area. It is a hollow body decoy made in the two piece method typical of the school. The carver is not known.

A drake Widgeon made by Mason's Decoy Factory in the Premier Grade.

This decoy was made by John Dawson of the Delaware River school. This drake Widgeon is a very good example of a bird from the school.

Mint condition hen and drake Pintails by Lem and Steve Ward. Extremely fine paint jobs are apparent on these classic 1936 models by the Ward Brothers.

A Pintail made by Charles "Shang" Wheeler about 1932. This very nice bird has much original paint, glass eyes, carved mandibles and face carving. The body is comb feather painted and the tail was fashioned from a piece of sheet copper.

An Ed Phillips drake Pintail. A solid body decoy with carved eyes and scratch feather painting. A beautifully carved and painted decoy by this Cambridge, Maryland commercial carver.

A Blue Wing Teal drake from the coast of Maine. This very small decoy was made in the 1920's or earlier but the identity of the maker is not known presently.

This pair of decoys
was made by the Mason's Decoy Factory.
They are Detroit Grade decoys
in the Blue Wing and Green Wing Teal species.

A two piece hollow body Brant decoy made by Ira
Hudson of Chincoteague, Virginia.

A very nice Ira Hudson Black Duck. Although it
doesn't have his typical "banjo tail" when you
examine this bird you can easily see his typical "flute
carving" in the tail.

This Redhead drake was made by the H. A. Stevens
Decoys company of Weedsport, New York. The very
nicely formed, flattish body and paddle tail are
typical of these factory decoys.

This nice Canada Goose was made by Ed Phillips of Cambridge, Maryland. Made as a "watch Gander" it is scratch feather painted and has a sheet lead ballast weight.

This is a Red Breasted Merganser made by the Wildfowler company. It bears the typical round brand or logo with the Quogue, Long Island location in it.

A Mason's Decoy Factory Challenge Grade drake Merganser in very good condition.

A hollow body
Canada Goose
made by Nathan Cobb.

Hooded Merganser drake
made by Ira Hudson of
the Virginia Eastern
Shore school of carvers.
This decoy illustrates the
"football body" and
"banjo tail" often used
by him.

Red Breasted Merganser
from the Maine school.
The carving and con-
struction details on this
decoy are typical of
Maine. It has an inletted
head and is strikingly
similar to that of decoys
by Gus Wilson but the
painting is more sophisticated than that normally
associated with Wilson's
products.

A Preier Grade drake Canvasback made by the Mason's Decoy Factory.

A Ward Brothers drake Canvasback in original paint. Sometimes known as the "Classic '36", it is carved from solid cedar and sports glass eyes.

An exceptionally nice Ira Hudson drake Canvasback decoy. Note the scalloped breast feather painting and "banjo tail" frequently used by Hudson.

VIRGINIA EASTERN SHORE

The majority of decoys from this region are of the solid-body, round bottom type with the remaining minority being hollow. There is quite a variety of types of decoys from this school; therefore the best way to familiarize you with them is to discuss a selected group of representative makers.

Ira Hudson of Chincoteague, Virginia, was the most prolific maker in the region. It is estimated that he produced over 20,000 decoys in his decoy-making days. Hudson made a number of different types, both solid and hollow-bodied. He was a commercial decoy maker and the type, style and sophistication of his products was largely dependent upon what his customers could afford. They ranged from very simply made and painted decoys to two- and three-piece hollow-bodied decoys with much detail carving, but the majority are solid-body. His choice of wood was white pine, but Hudson decoys have been found in cedar, cypress, balsa and cottonwood. Eyes were generally tack eyes or painted. He seldom utilized glass eyes. He often used the scratch feather painting technique. Carved neck notches or "thumbprint carving" are sometimes found on the back behind the neck.

In all the variations in type of decoy his painting technique and style remained constant and after handling and studying several the collector should be able to readily recognize it. The photos accompanying show a representative range of his decoy styles.

The usual method Hudson used to attach head to body was to place the neck down into a carved out hollow, although he utilized other methods such as the neck shelf carving. Hudson is also noted for using unusual head positions. Not always, but much of the time he accomplished this by carving the heads from driftwood or roots.

Dave "Umbrella" Watson was a commercial maker from Chincoteague, Virginia, whose style was a blend of Eastern Shore Virginia and New Jersey construction and styles, easily distinguished from the New Jersey decoys by the presence of delicate raised wing and tail carving detail. The Watson decoy is of two-piece hollow body usually. A reasonable estimate of each would be 90 percent hollow and 10 percent solid body. The decoys were well sanded before painting. The painting was always well done and all his birds sport glass eyes placed in a carved eye groove. Most are carved from white cedar in two halves joined above the waterline.

Miles Hancock's decoys were all solid body, constructed with flat bottoms. Most of his decoys were carved from cottonwood, a soft, easy to carve wood. He first roughed the shape out then did his finishing with pieces of broken glass. He never sanded them before painting and his painting technique was not very refined. The result of this is rough but surprisingly effective overall. He supposedly never used glass eyes, sticking to tack eyes exclusively. There have been a few to show up with glass eyes, but these may have been later replacements by the users.

Charles Birch of Willis Wharf, Virginia, made decoys that were quite similar to New Jersey decoys in the general overall look of them. His decoys were the two-piece hollow body mostly with a few solid decoys that still had the appearance of being hollow-bodied. There are two significant variances from the New Jersey decoys that make them easily identifiable as Birch products. All his decoys will have a definite flat spot on the top of the body about three-fourths of the length back from the breast toward the tail. Another distinctive detail is the use of a reinforcing wooden dowel peg inserted from the bottom and visible from there.

Birch always used a shelf carving to receive the head, nailed on pad weights and his geese and swans had inletted oak or hickory bills. The latter were inserted fully through the head and tightened in the back of the head by driving a spline into a split at that end of the bill piece. See map on page 34.

Value Ranges for Eastern Shore Virginia Decoys

Ira Hudson .... $500 - 1200
Dave "Umbrella" Watson .... 250 - 500
Doug Jester .... 250 - 450
Charles Birch .... 400 - 1200
Miles Hancock .... 200 - 500

PLATE 84. Hooded Merganser drake by Ira Hudson. This decoy illustrates the "football body" and "banjo tail" often used by him. Note the fluted carving on the tail, characteristic of many of his more elaborately carved birds. Tack eyes and bill carving are also present.

PLATE 85. An Ira Hudson Black Duck. Although this decoy does not have the "banjo tail", the fluted carving can be readily seen. A very fine example of scratch-feather painting.

PLATE 86. This is a very typical Ira Hudson Scaup decoy. The high crown head and flattened breast characteristics are common to his decoys of this species. They are often found with "banjo tails". The usual local name in the Virginia Eastern Shore area for this species is "Blackhead".

PLATE 87. An exceptional Ira Hudson Canvasback drake in original paint. Note the scalloped breast feather painting and "banjo tail" often used by Hudson.

PLATE 88. This Brant by Ira Hudson has a two-piece hollow body with the joint above the waterline. Note the neck notch or "thumbprint carving" behind the neck and the carved shelf neck attachment.

PLATE 89. This hissing Canada Goose decoy made by Ira Hudson has a solid body but they are also found with hollow bodies.

PLATE 90. A Black Duck by Dave "Umbrella" Watson that is a very good illustration of the characteristics of a typical Watson decoy. Glass eyes in a carved eye groove; slight amount of delicate raised wing carving; and the above-the-waterline joint of the two-piece hollow body.

PLATE 91. A drake Blackhead made by Ira Hudson of Chincoteague, Virginia.

PLATE 92. Widgeon drake by Miles Hancock of Chincoteague, Virginia.

PLATE 93. Doug Jester Black Duck decoy. Jester is in the Virginia Eastern Shore School.

PLATE 94. Miles Hancock swimming Canada Goose. This flat-bottomed rough finished decoy is carved from native Virginia cottonwood; body, neck and head. It has tack eyes and is almost crude in painting; nevertheless it comes up rather nicely as you can readily see.

PLATE 95. Another decoy by Miles Hancock. This drake Widgeon is a very good example of how hurried the painting of his birds usually look. Notice, however, the use of scratch feather painting so common to decoys of the Virginia Eastern Shore.

PLATE 96. A Brant by Miles Hancock. Solid cottonwood with tack eyes and typical crude paint pattern.

PLATE 97. Black Duck by Charles Birch of Willis Wharf on the Eastern Shore of Virginia. It has a very prominent shelf carving to receive the neck, tack eyes and has a two-piece hollow cedar body, as do most of his birds.

PLATE 98. This drake Canvasback is another Charles Birch decoy. The above-the-waterline joint for the two halves of the hollow body can be easily seen in this photo. Exhibits typical Birch characteristics.

PLATE 99. A Canada Goose by Charles Birch. This fine decoy has a shelf carving, tack eyes, inletted hardwood bill, reinforcing wooden dowel peg and is a two-piece hollow-bodied.

PLATE 100. A solid body Black Duck made by Doug Jester. This typical Jester decoy has scratch feather painting. As so many of the good Virginia Eastern Shore makers were, Doug Jester was from Chincoteague. He always made solid body birds with shelf carving for the neck and head. The mandibles always had some carving details. This decoy has no eyes, but the horizontal line in the eye area is frequently seen on his products.

COBB ISLAND

Cobb Island, off the Eastern Shore of Virginia, is now uninhabited but was the home of the Cobb family. Nathan Cobb and his family settled on the island in 1833 as the result of a shipwreck. The family had sailed south from New England and whatever their destination originally had been, the island (subsequently named after them) became their home. The decoys they made were unlike those of other Eastern Shore Virginia makers. They apparently adhered to the methods that were common to the area of their former home. Their decoys are much like those of Massachusetts.

Many of the Cobb Island decoys are found with the initial "N" or "E" and an occasional "A" carved on the bottom. The initials are of Nathan, Jr., Elkenah and Albert or Arthur.

Generally the decoys were made slightly oversize and they are two-piece hollow body mostly, but some were solid body. The ballast weights were sheet or flattened lead and always attached with brass screws. Head and neck is inletted into the hollow body. It is significant to note that inletting into **hollow** bodies is unusual. Frequently this inletted head and neck includes a portion of the breast as well. The bills on the greater proportion of the Cobb family's larger species of birds are inletted into the head. Made of hardwood they extend all the way through the head and are splined at the back of the head. You may note that Charles Birch of the Virginia Eastern Shore practiced this, but he was a later maker and probably emulated the Cobbs.

The Cobb birds are particularly noted for the many different life-like attitudes of heads; each decoy being different. This was accomplished by their extensive use of roots or driftwood to fashion the heads.

The decoys are usually flat bottomed but some are found with round bottoms.

Split wing/tail carving is common to their birds, as is the use of glass eyes. There are, however, a goodly number with no eye representation at all.

Painting was life-like and effective but lack sophisticated detailing.

There have been some extraordinarily high prices realized at auction, but most average decoys from the Cobb family would be valued between $500 and $1500. See map on page 34.

PLATE 101. Black Duck made by Nathan Cobb Jr. around 1870. It has a two-piece hollow white cedar body and pine head with glass eyes. Head, neck and portion of breast is inletted. The split tail, wing carving and sheet lead ballast weight attached with brass screws completes the list of typical Cobb black duck decoys.

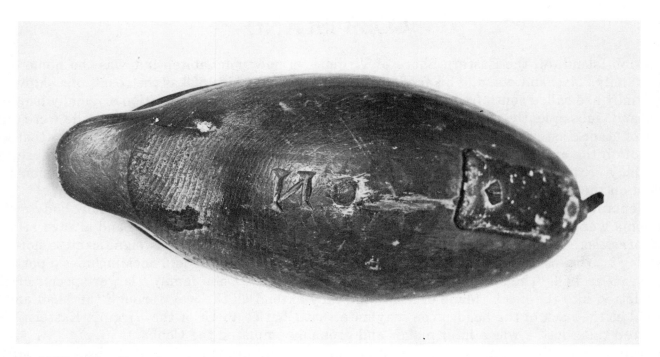

PLATE 102. Bottom view of the Nathan Cobb Black Duck in Plate 101 showing the sheet lead ballast weight and the initial brand "N". The photo is not printed reversed. The crossbar in the "N" is actually carved backwards on the decoy.

PLATE 103. This Black Duck made by Elkenah Cobb exhibits all of the typical Cobb characteristics discussed in the caption for Plate 101. Note that the carving style differs a bit. Elkenah Cobb apparently didn't carve his birds with the high rounded back typical of his father Nathan's decoys.

PLATE 104. A bottom view of the Elkenah Cobb Black Duck decoy showing his initial brand "E".

PLATE 105. This pre-Civil War Canada Goose was made by Nathan Cobb Jr. It has an inletted head/neck, typical split tail/wing carving and is two-piece hollow bodied. The head has glass eyes and an inletted hardwood bill.

PLATE 106. A close-up view of the back of the head of the Canada Goose in Plate 105 showing the peg-end of the inletted bill. If you look closely, you can see the spline that was driven into the end. This technique is discussed in more detail in the accompanying text on Cobb Island decoys.

PLATE 107. This is a **solid** body Brant decoy made by a member of the Cobb family. It has a very nice locust root head with an inletted bill. In this case, the entire face is inletted, not just the bill.

PLATE 108. Bottom view of the Brant in Plate 107. Note the hole in the bottom. This enabled the decoy to be used as a stick-up field decoy as well as a floater.

PLATE 109. A Cobb family Brant decoy in a style slightly different from the norm. It is a round bottom solid body bird with the typical root head and split wing/tail. Note the hole in the side of the breast. The hole on each side was for the insertion of a brass, copper or bronze wire bent in a shape similar to a doctor's stethoscope. Weighted at the bottom, this device imparted a bobbing motion with wave action, resulting in a very life-like simulation of a feeding Brant.

NORTH CAROLINA

This school of carvers also includes a portion of Virginia just north of the state line called Back Bay. The decoys of the Back Bay area and those of coastal North Carolina are indistinguishable for the most part.

The North Carolina School is particularly noted for its slightly oversize Ruddy Ducks. They have been called crude by many, but the overall appearance of most examples is pleasing. The most striking feature of the decoys is the very nicely shaped head on them. None are finely finished but still they are effective. Eyes are usually not present or simply painted on.

Most makers concentrated on solid body, round or semi-'V' bottom decoys. One exception are the decoys of Ned Burgess who made his birds with flat bottoms.

There were wire frame Geese and Swans made in the region. Although they do appear to be very nice decoys in the accompanying plates, they would have to be considered somewhat crude if compared to one made by Massachusetts maker Joe Lincoln.

A significant characteristic common to most North Carolina decoys is the type of anchor line tie used. If you glance at the decoys in the accompanying photographs, you will note most of them have a prominent nail protruding from the lower portion of the breast. Less obvious is the actual line tie somewhere below and behind. The purpose of the breast nail is to provide a means of lengthening or shortening the anchor line. This was necessary because of the large tide fluctuations in the area. The hunter could choose his length by using a half-hitch to the nail and letting the extra line simply hang beneath the decoy.

A ballast weight that was often used in the Back Bay and upper North Carolina area is shown on the decoy in Plate 113. See map on page 39.

Value Ranges for North Carolina Decoys

Lem and Lee Dudley . . . . $600 - 2500
Ned Burgess . . . . 100 - 400

PLATE 110. This stately looking Canvasback from North Carolina was made by Alvira Wright from Duck, North Carolina. It is a big heavy solid body bird with a rather massive ballast weight. In spite of this the bird floats only about one and one-half inches deep. Wright was also a boat builder. His decoys obviously reflect his skill and knowledge of the craft.

PLATE 111. A Ned Burgess Ruddy Duck. Burgess was from Church's Island, Virginia, and is the exception to makers of his school in that he generally produced **flat** bottom decoy. Note the prominent nail protruding from the breast. This North Carolina School characteristic is discussed in the accompanying text.

PLATE 112. This classic North Carolina Ruddy Duck is from Knott's Island. The maker is not known.

PLATE 113. A Ned Burgess Canvasback that has never been hunted over. It bears a ballast weight typically used in the upper portion of the North Carolina School. This particular weight has the initials "NPW" cast into the surface. The initials are of Nelson Price Whittaker who ran a foundry that made, among other things, ballast weights and cast iron wing decoys.

PLATE 114. A very nice Lee or Lem Dudley Ruddy Duck. The brothers were from Knott's Island, North Carolina. Note the typical protruding nail and cast weight. They always cast their own weights.

PLATE 115. This is a bottom view of the Dudley Ruddy Duck in Plate 114. It is difficult to see, but the "LD" brand the Dudleys almost always used on their decoys is above the ballast weight.

PLATE 116. An extremely nice wire framed canvas-covered Swan decoy. The maker is not known but it is from the Currituck Island, North Carolina, area.

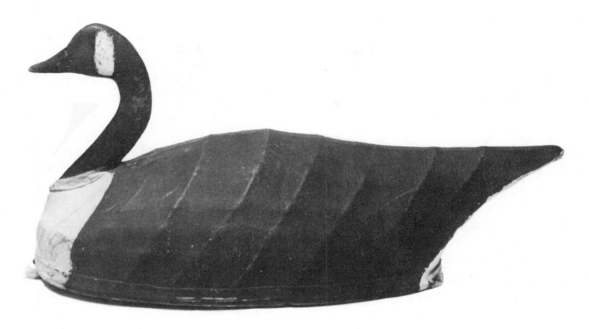

PLATE 117. A wire frame, canvas covered Canada Goose made by Ned Burgess. North Carolina is one of the very few places where the wire frame construction technique was used.

PLATE 118. Wire frame, canvas covered Swan made by Manny Haywood of Kill Devil Hill, North Carolina. Haywood used glass eyes in his Swan decoys.

SOUTH CAROLINA

Up to now no books and few periodicals have paid much attention to decoys from South Carolina. This omission is understandable when you consider how few documented South Carolina decoys have been found and added to private collections. On the other hand it is difficult to understand once you have seen the few that have so far been uncovered, for they are striking in beauty, style and size.

The origin of these decoys is still a bit hazy, but so far research in the area indicates that a family from around Georgetown, South Carolina, named Cains is responsible for some of them. There were at least two Cains brothers, Hucks and Saynay Cains and possibly a third, Bob, who produced the decoys. One of them is known to have worked for Bernard Baruch on his plantation, Hobcaw Barony. Indeed some decoys attributed to the Cains brothers bear Baruch's brand "BMB".

The most handsome of these decoys have an unmistakable style about them. The head and neck of the Mallards are gracefully carved in what is described as a "snakey neck" with elongated bills and carved eyes. The head and neck are carved from one piece of wood and the body is of solid one-piece construction. Usually made of Tupelo gum or cypress, they have raised wing carving and, if you view just about any of them from above, you will note a distinctive heart shape formed by the wing carving.

Some of the decoys, particularly Black Ducks, are hollow bodied and often have glass eyes. It should be noted here that it appears some of the Mallard decoys appear to have been repainted as Black Ducks, and vice versa.

There have been no trade data sufficient to establish values found, but once you have had the opportunity to personally examine these particular South Carolina decoys you will have no problem knowing that they are extremely valuable.

PLATE 119. Hen Mallard decoy attributed to Hucks Cains. The grace, beauty and style of carving of this South Carolina decoy is unsurpassed. As are all the South Carolina decoys, this one is painted with much detail in dull muted colors.

PLATE 120. This Mallard drake is the mate to the hen in Plate 119. The wing carving of these decoys, when viewed from above result in the heart shape characteristic of the Cains Mallards. The numerous more or less vertical marks on the body are the result of wrapping the anchor line around the decoy during storage and transport.

PLATE 121. This rather strange looking hen Mallard is attributed to Hucks Cains. It is speculated that this decoy represents one of the earliest attempts at decoy making by the Cains brothers. The narrow portion of the back is obviously made to facilitate anchor line storage.

PLATE 122. This swimming or feeding Black Duck is attributed to the Cains brothers because of the unmistakable heart shape formed by the wing carving. This decoy probably represents mid-range in the evolution of Cains Brothers decoy making. Although it is not clear in the photograph, this decoy has no eye representation.

PLATE 123. Although most of the decoys are carved with raised wings, this Mallard drake is referred to as the "raised wing" variety.

PLATE 124. A hollow-body Black Duck. It has glass eyes and the two-piece hollow body is joined at a point above the waterline.

PLATE 125. This is a bottom view of the Black Duck in Plate 124, showing the "BMB" brand of Bernard M. Baruch. So far all the decoys with his brand have been hollow bodied.

PLATE 126. This Bob Cains decoy shot from above shows a definite heart shape. This heart shape resulting from the raised wing carving is a typical characteristic of Cains Brothers birds.

PLATE 127. Blue Wing Teal attributed to Bob Cains. This decoy can be considered fairly rare because it is the only species other than Black Ducks and Mallards that have been attributed to the Cains Brothers. It is rather elaborately painted, using the scratch feather technique. There are only four of these presently known to be in private collections. The eyes are glass hat pins.

LOUISIANA

Commercial makers produced thousands upon thousands of decoys, running the gamut from crude chunks of wood, decoys painted as if for a carnival midway to superb highly detailed and beautifully painted birds. It seems that everybody and his brother were making decoys. Louisiana makers probably produced a wider variety of species of wildfowl decoys than any other single region in the United States. It is therefore next to impossible to provide the collector with anything more than the broadest generalizations in describing any common characteristics for Louisiana decoys.

There are between fifteen and twenty makers from the Louisiana area that are most popularly collected, but to further complicate the identification and valuation problems, the majority of these decoys reside in just a small number of private collections, most of which belong to Louisiana collectors and, further, there is precious little trade data for the decoys are seldom put on public sale.

A few of the better known makers are Victor Alfonzo, Adam Ansardi, Xavier Bourg, Domingue Campo, Alcide Carmadel, Jack and Robert Couret, William Duet, Gaston Isadore, Dewey Pertuit, Rome Roussell, Nicole Vidacovich, Cadis Vizier, Mark Whipple, and the products of the loose partnership of three men who worked cooperatively, George Frederick, Charles Joefrau and Mitchel LaFrance.

The decoys in the accompanying photographs are by the members of the group of popularly collected Louisiana Carvers.

If you have an interest in collecting decoys from Louisiana, it is strongly recommended that you obtain two books. **Decoys of the Mississippi Flyway** by Alan G. Haid has a large, excellent section of photographs of Louisiana decoys; and **Louisiana Duck Decoys** by Charles W. Frank Jr.

Values range quite widely and there seem to be little available trade data with which one could establish realistic ranges. A hazardous guess might place an average Louisiana decoy in the $100 - 200 range. This would of course except those highly sought examples and the low value, rather crude examples as well.

PLATE 128. A drake Mallard made by Alcide Carmadel. Made of cypress in solid body type with a rooty looking head and upswept tail, this is not a particularly good overall example of his decoys but the shape of the body is typical. His heads were usually rendered much nicer than this one.

PLATE 129. A very nice Bluewing Teal drake by Xavier Bourg from Larose, Louisiana. Solid body with well carved raised wings and tack eyes.

ILLINOIS RIVER

The Illinois River school boasts some of the nicest hollow body working decoys to be found in the country. The norm was to construct them in two pieces that were hollowed out and then joined at a point above the waterline. They were carved realistically with much fine bill and face detail. Some of them even have hollow necks and heads. Just about all have glass eyes. Frequently the commercial makers would have ballast weights made for them with their names cast into the strip lead weight surface, making their products easily identified if the original weight is present.

Most of the decoys have a rounded semi-'V' bottom. Many of them have been found with a coat of shellac or varnish. It is theorized that they felt, because the waters they hunted in were usually muddy or murky, that an orange shellac made them more visible to the live bird.

The Mallard decoy is the most commonly found species in the area for that was the dominant bird in the Mississippi Flyway.

Painting was very realistic with the comb feather painting technique frequently applied.

Value Ranges for Illinois River Decoys

Robert Elliston
    Range for average decoys .... $200 - 1000
    Range for extraordinary decoys .... 800 - 2500
Bert Graves .... 250 - 1250
Perry Wilcoxen .... 150 - 500
Charles Perdew .... 500 - 2000

These ranges are all for quite good condition decoys.

PLATE 130. An Illinois River Mallard drake decoy made by J. Fred Mott Sr. around 1898. It is a two-piece hollow body bird with tack eyes and a shelf carving to receive the head/neck. Mott, Sr. was from Pekin, Illinois.

PLATE 131. This Illinois River decoy is a drake Mallard made by Perry Wilcoxen of Liverpool, Illinois. Typical two-piece hollow body construction with shelf carving.

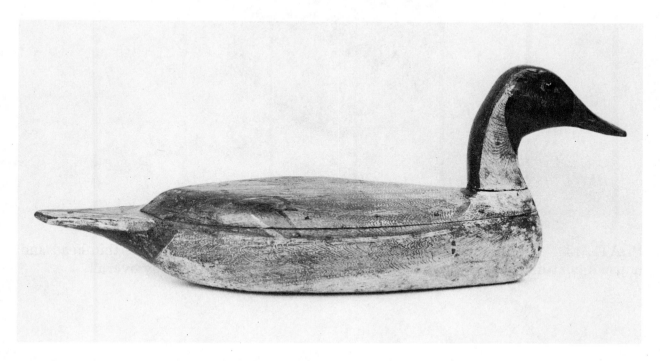

PLATE 132. A nicely shaped Illinois River drake Pintail. Maker unknown.

PLATE 133. Front view of the above Illinois River Pintail showing the thin head and unusual boat-like shape of the body. A very gracefully shaped decoy overall.

PLATE 134. Pintail Duck made by William T. Shaw of Macon, Illinois. Quite typical Illinois River decoy with glass eyes, two-piece hollow body and strip lead ballast weight. The "S" brand visible in the photo was used by Shaw to identify his products. Note the tail carving detail.

PLATE 135. The maker of this Illinois River Scaup drake is not known, but it is another nice example of decoys from the School. It has a typical strip lead weight that bears the inscription "Raymond Lead Company". This company was located in Chicago, Illinois.

MICHIGAN

Decoys from this school comprise two types. One type was made for hunting in the heavy waters of the Great Lakes and the other are those made for use in more calm waters and shallow marshes.

The Great Lakes decoys were made large with hollow bodies and big keels. They were generally hollowed out from the bottom and closed up with bottom boards. There are lots of unusual keels to be found on Michigan decoys some of them being downright ingenious. The other type are constructed in the same manner but are usually smaller in scale, lack the large heavy keels and use a very thin bottom board. By the time decoy making had worked its way this far West from the Atlantic seaboard, it was about 1880. Makers of this part of the country had the experience of their Eastern predecessors from which to draw on, many sources for fine materials and good tools available to work with. The band saw and glass eyes are two good examples of this. It is therefore no surprise that the decoys of the Mid-West are for the most part very finely made and finished. Just about all decoys from the region have good quality glass eyes. Most are hollow body types with bottom boards, but there are some very nice solid body birds to be found as well. Some makers also used cork in fashioning bodies and mounted them on bottom boards for stability and durability.

As a whole the decoys of the region are beautifully constructed and painted. The collector would do well to concentrate his efforts in the whole region including Michigan, the St. Clairs Flats, Illinois River, etc. There are probably quite a few decoys as yet not found and there were a few makers who are known to have produced literally thousands of them in their combined carving careers.

The value range for good to excellent decoys made by Ben Schmidt would be from $145 to $500. Most of the others in the school would follow the range fairly closely.

PLATE 136. This beautifully constructed and painted c. 1925 Canvasback drake was made by Walter Strubling of Marine City, Michigan. It is surprisingly light relative to its large size and heavy looking construction. It is hollow bodied with a 5/8" bottom board and has a very large swing type keel. This keel is very like the swinging keels designed for ease of trailering some small to medium sailboats so common today. The bottom board and keel are attached by means of countersunk brass marine screws. It has glass eyes, fine head and bill carving details and a thick heavy well executed paint pattern. Made for hunting in heavy water such as might be encountered often in the Great Lakes.

PLATE 137. A bottom view of the decoy shown in Plate 136 with the swing keel extended as it would be when floating.

PLATE 138. A Black Duck made by Ben Schmidt of Detroit, Michigan. Slightly smaller than the Strubling Canvasback in Plate 136 this decoy could serve double duty as a big water decoy because of its fairly sizable keel but it was likely made for use in more shallow water and marshes at the edge of the lakes and even in the smaller bodies of water such as Lake St. Clair. This decoy like just about all decoys made by Ben Schmidt has a solid body, glass eyes, and very good raised wing carving details. Schmidt used a very unique method of making feather representations on the bodies of his birds. He shaped his own tool for stamping crescent shaped feather details into the bodies. Some hollow body Schmidt decoys are found though the majority are solid.

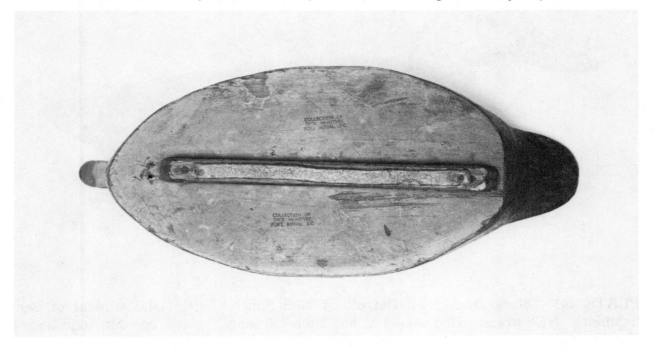

PLATE 139. This bottom view of the Schmidt Black Duck in Plate 138 illustrates the typical keel and strip lead weight he used.

129

PLATE 140. A hen Canvasback attributed to Ben Schmidt of Detroit.

PLATE 141. Black Duck from Detroit by Neil Smith (friend and student of Ben Schmidt). NES brand. Had a keel at one time full length of flat bottom, solid body; glass eyes; nice bill and face carving; raised wing. Same stamped feather technique developed by Schmidt. c. 1952.

ST. CLAIR FLATS

For the most part decoys from the banks of St. Clair Flats are very light, well constructed flat-bottom, hollow-body birds with thin bottom boards (some as thin as 1/4 inch). Some even boast hollow necks and heads. They are finely sanded and finished, sporting glass eyes. There were many fine lowheads and sleepers made in the area.

Lake St. Clair is on the United States and Canadian border with the border running north/south through the lake. There are, therefore, American and Canadian carvers in the school. Serious collectors divide the St. Clair Flats into two separate schools, the Toronto School and the Mount Clemons School. The accompanying photographs are of decoys by makers from both sides of the lake, but for our purposes we will not differentiate any further. The differences are definite but subtle and not within the purview of this basic guide.

Value Range for St. Clair Flats Decoys in Excellent Condition: $200 - 600.

PLATE 142. A very nice Redhead drake by Canadian St. Clair Flats maker Thomas Chambers. A very typical decoy from this school, it is a flat-bottom hollow body bird with a thin bottom board. It has glass eyes and excellent detailed mandible carving. The carved diamond-shape nostrils is an identifying characteristic of Thomas Chambers decoys.

PLATE 143. View of the bottom of the Thomas Chambers Redhead in Plate 142, showing various brands. The important one to note here is "THOS CHAMBERS". If you look close toward the lower side in the photo of the bottom, you can see the "K" that is part of the word "MAKER".

PLATE 144. This is a very nice and very old Canvasback by Tobin Meldren (Meldrum in some references) of Fairhaven, Michigan, on the far northern shore of Lake St. Clair. Typical hollow body decoy with thin bottom board and glass eyes. This decoy would delight any collector of folk art as well as the collector of St. Clair Flats School decoys.

PLATE 145. A very small hollow-body bottom board St. Clair Flats decoy with glass eyes and nice bill and face carving. Very little original paint left on the decoy whose maker is unknown.

PLATE 146. A St. Clair Flats drake Redhead by Thomas Chambers.

PLATE 147. This is a solid body, glass eye drake Canvasback by Ralph Reghi. This particular decoy was used on the St. Clair Flats but differs from the norm. It represents a smaller group of carvers that made their birds in the Mount Clemons style. Mount Clemons is just north of Detroit on the northwestern side of Lake St. Clair.

PLATE 148. This is a later Tom Schroeder drake Redhead. His earlier hollow-body birds were typical St. Clair Flats decoys. This one is in the same style but is a solid body composition with a wooden head.

WISCONSIN

With the exception of factory-made decoys, there were few commercial makers in the Wisconsin School. Most of the decoys of the area were made by the individual hunters for themselves and perhaps a few for friends. There were nevertheless many, many fine decoys made in Wisconsin.

Decoys from this school are generally oversize renditions of diving duck species. They are usually found in solid-body construction, but there are some very nice hollow-body examples to be found as well. Whatever the construction technique, they all usually have exaggerated body features such as big, long necks and hump backs.

Paint styles or patterns are usually very similar to factory birds widely used in the Midwest.

Value Ranges for Wisconsin Decoys

John McKinney	$150 - 325
Gus Moak	300 - 650
Frank Strey	50 - 250

PLATE 149. This hen Canvasback is from Wisconsin, but the maker is not presently known. It is quite similar to those made by August Moak and Joseph Sieger of the Wisconsin School.

PLATE 150. A drake Canvasback, mate to the hen in Plate 149. Both have glass eyes and paint patterns imilar to factory-made decoys of the Midwest. Both exhibit the hump backs and long necks discussed in the accompanying text. It must have proved quite a problem to transport and deploy more than six or eight of these large, heavy solid body decoys. Both show much repair, lending evidence to their susceptibility to damage in handling.

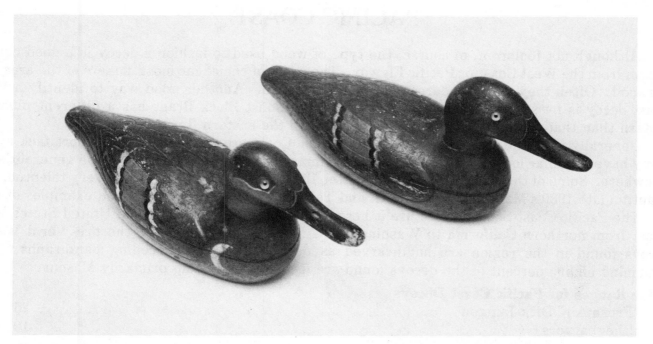

PLATE 151. A beautiful little pair of Greenwing Teals from Wisconsin. The maker of these decoys is not known. They are two-piece hollow body decoys with glass eyes and finely carved face and bill and feather details. A lot of Wisconsin birds are found with small brass or copper tags with the owner's name and address inscribed.

PLATE 152. A c. 1930 drake Redhead made by Frank Strey of Oshkosh, Wisconsin. Strey's decoys were heavy over-sized solid body birds. They generally have good face and bill carving details although the amount and attention to this carving diminished as the years went by. The bodies also have varying degrees of rasp work. Glass eyes and flat bottoms complete the list of typical characteristics of the birds from the hands of this Wisconsin School carver.

PACIFIC COAST

Although not foolproof, of course, the type of wood used to fashion a decoy is a good clue to decoys from the West Coast or Pacific Flyway. The wood of choice for most makers of the area was redwood. Often they used ponderosa pine for heads also. Another good way to identify a West Coast decoy is by species. For instance, the Pacific Coast Black Brant has a different plumage pattern than that of the Brant that migrates through the eastern flyways.

Generally the hand-carved decoys of the Pacific Coast are solid bodied and sport tack eyes. Many have a similar look about them. There are many notable exceptions to these generalities as elsewhere. Some of the makers who worked after 1900 (some still carving) were very talented. The beautiful late 1930's Mallards, Canvasback and Teals of Harry H. Cook are good examples of this.

The Pacific Coast School as we use it here encompassed the whole of the United States West Coast from northern California to Washington. About twenty percent of the pre-World War II decoys found in the region are hand-carved as described in the preceding paragraphs. The remaining eighty percent of the decoys found are factory-made being primarily Masons.

Value Ranges for Pacific Coast Decoys

"Fresh Air" Dick Jantzen .... 250 - 600
Other carvers .... 100 - 750

PLATE 153. The maker of this Pacific Coast Black Brant is not known. It is an excellent representation of West Coast decoys of the species. It is solid body constructed of redwood, has tack eyes, and is rigged with line ties fore and aft. It is a 1920's decoy from the Northern Coast of California.

PLATE 154. This is a hen Pintail made by Dick "Fresh Air" Jantzen of California. His birds represent some of the really nice decoys to be found on the West Coast. This particular one was hollowed out by drilling out through the breast area.

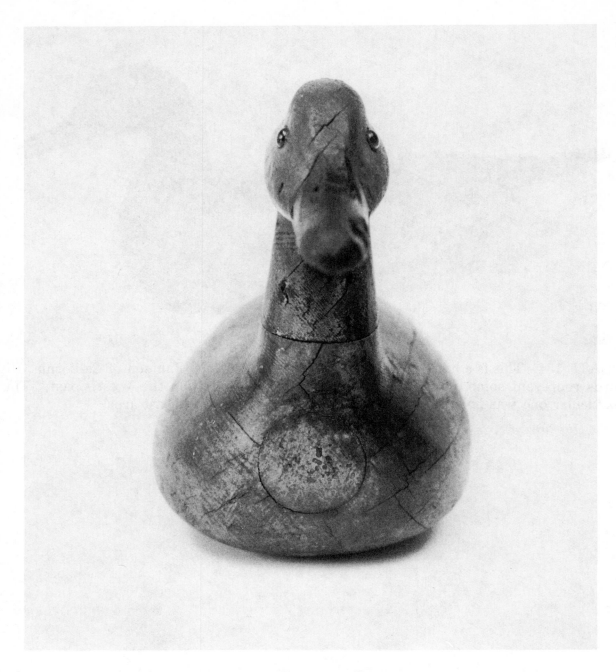

PLATE 155. A front view of the above Jantzen Pintail showing the plug where the decoy was drilled out from. Jantzen did not always use this method.

FACTORY DECOYS

During the last half of the 1800's the popularity of sport hunting increased dramatically. This coupled with the appearance of the market hunter, his requisite large rigs of decoys and the advent of the duplicating lathe made it economically feasible for the establishment of factories for the commercial manufacture of decoys. There were established hundreds of operations, a few of which became large and successful. There were also several small operations to achieve success.

The use of the word "factory" can be misleading as used here. It does indeed describe large operations such as Mason's Decoy Factory, but here we are also including any commercial operation location devoted to the manufacture of wooden decoys in which the duplicating lathe is an integral part of their production, or the production, lathe or no, was on an assembly line basis. This latter could encompass many. many makers, but only those who have been routinely accepted as factory decoys by collectors are included. Most of these have been accepted as "factories" by virtue of extensive commercial advertising of the decoys.

Factory made decoys made by the most well known companies were all quite similar to each other. Excepting the Stevens and Victor Animal Trap Companies, who came along before Mason's Decoy Factory, it appears that most of the better known factory decoys made were influenced by Mason products. Mason and probably many others would, however, make atypical decoys on special order but their regular lines all performed their tasks in pretty much the same manner in most conditions. Therefore a small degree of standardization was practiced, albeit by accident.

Manufacturing operations were in a position to make innovations in decoys not practical to hand makers. Some of the innovations such as the folding tin shorebird decoys were successful and some were little more than comical. A decoy that flapped its wings was once patented; a dubious achievement at best.

The metal bodied decoys with wood bottom boards and the folding tin shorebirds had appeared by the mid-1860's and rubber decoys arrived about 1867. There were even some "honking" decoys produced by factories.

The art of the manufactured wooden decoy, however, was carried to its highest form by the early factories and this is what they finally concentrated their efforts on.

The collector can encounter factory decoys just about anywhere for they were made by the thousands (especially around Detroit) and shipped to just about all points of the compass. A notable exception is New England. There seems to be a shortage of factory made decoys in that part of the country. Conjecture leads us to think the reason is the reputation New Englanders have of being handy, educated in fine craftsmanship, industrious and possessing innate "Yankee ingenuity". In short, they probably thought "Anything they can do, we can do better" and proceeded to make their own, shunning store bought decoys.

While hunting for factory decoys it might be judicious to keep in mind another theoretical possibility. It would not be unreasonable to think that some employees of factories carried their vocation home and made decoys in home workshops. There were many talented people working in these factories (especially painters) and there would be nothing to prevent them from making decoys. It is most reasonable to assume some of them might have produced birds that were almost, if not completely, identical to the factory product. I can't pretend to advise you what to do or think about this possibility but am compelled to point it out to you.

The new wildfowl laws of 1918 struck a fatal blow to the manufacturing companies, and factory after factory went out of business almost overnight. The laws eliminated the market hunters, thus their huge demand for decoys simply vanished.

J. N. DODGE

Jasper N. Dodge of Detroit, Michigan, went to business in 1884 when he bought an existing decoy making operation owned by George Peterson. The Peterson products were very fine, usually solid body birds with glass eyes. Although Dodge didn't use Peterson's original patterns, he did utilize many of the existing techniques. His were also generally solid bodied but, like Peterson, he also manufactured some hollow decoys in the St. Clair Flats style.

Early Dodge decoys had unusual eyes. The eye hole was drilled out and a tack placed in the hole, resulting in slightly recessed tack eyes that appeared very much like glass eyes. Later he adopted the glass eyes. Dodge also carried on the breast swirl style of painting developed by Peterson. This swirl style was later used extensively by the Mason's Decoy Factory in Detroit.

Dodge advertised that he would make decoys ". . . after any model furnished without extra charge". It is therefore possible to find many different types, styles and species made by the company.

Value Ranges for J. N. Dodge Decoys

Merganser and Canada Goose .... $300 - 500
Other Species .... 75 - 200

PLATE 156. A very early original paint Canada Goose by J. N. Dodge. This bird probably dates prior to about 1890. It has great original paint for its age, nice bill carving and the recessed tack eyes discussed in the accompanying text.

PLATE 157. A later model decoy by J. N. Dodge. This hen Scaup has no bill and face carving. Glass eyes were the rule in these later birds, but most significant is the swirl paint pattern on the breast. See text discussion.

EVANS DUCK DECOY COMPANY

Walter Evans of Ladysmith, Wisconsin, began making decoys in 1921 and continued in business only until 1932 when illness forced him to cease operation. From beginning to end the Evans Duck Decoy Company was essentially a one-man operation with two duplicating lathes that turned out decoy bodies one at a time each. He offered three different types or grades of decoy in various species. The largest grade, the "Mammoth", was offered only in solid bodies but the other two, the "Standard" and "Competitive" were offered in both solid and hollow bodies. The "Competitive" grade was not sanded but rather left with the ridged lathe blade marks around the body. The others were very nicely sanded and finished.

The hollow bodies were fashioned by two different methods. One is the familiar two-piece hollow body, in two more or less equal halves, but the other method was rather unusual. He would take a solid body and drill a one and one-fourth inch hole through the front of the breast longitudinally into the body. He then plugged the hole in front and finished the bird.

All heads were hand carved and sported quality glass eyes. His method of preparing his decoys for painting was effective, rendering the finish very durable. Many are found today with very good original paint as a result.

The decoys have a Mason look to them and, indeed, it is said that he was inspired to go into the business of decoy making after finding a Mason premier grade Mallard and, being a woodworker by trade, deciding that he could do as well.

Evans frequently rubber stamped the words "Evans Decoy" on the bottom of these flat bottom decoys. This stamp is not always found as he, like most other makers, individuals or factories, wasn't particularly diligent in placing his brand on his products.

Numbers of birds he produced are not known, but a widely circulated photograph of him at work in his shop pictures about 150 Mallard and Canvasback decoys in various stages of completion. With this evidence it can reasonably be assumed that in ten or eleven years he must have produced at least a minimum of one thousand decoys, perhaps many more.

The collector value range for Evans decoys run from $100 to $500.

PLATE 158. A drake Bluebill or Scaup made by the Evans Duck Decoy Company of Ladysmith, Wisconsin. Hollow body with glass eyes.

PLATE 159. Front view of the Scaup decoy in Plate 158 showing the plug in the breast. This seals off the 1¼ inch hole made by Evans' unusual method of hollowing out the body of some of his decoys. Discussed in further detail in the accompanying text.

PLATE 160. Bottom view of the Scaup in Plate 159 showing the rubber stamped brand frequently found on Evans decoys.

HERTERS, INC.

Many of the Herters early decoys are desirable to collectors but by far the most highly sought are the Owl and Crow decoys. They made the best Owls of any of the others. Their Owls, for instance, usually exceed one thousand dollars when put up at auction.

The beaks of the Owls are actually made from Grizzly Bear claws.

Most of their birds found today have solid balsa bodies and cedar heads.

The company is still located in Waseca, Minnesota. The collectible decoys from Herters date around the 1930's and 1940's, with some fairly desirable ones being made in the 1960's.

Herters marketed some birds in the late 1960's and early 1970's under the name "Ancient Wooden Decoys" which were not decoys at all. They were Wood ducks, Mergansers, Mallards, etc., that were flat bottomed, not rigged and not keeled. They were made for decorative purposes only. They are branded "Herters' 1893". This is reference only to the year the company was founded.

The collector value range for Herters decoys is $50 to $250.

PLATE 161. A Herters' Great Horned Owl and a Crow. The "V" shape notch in the base of the Owl is made to receive and hold a dead crow decoy, thereby making it look as if the owl had killed it. Owls are deadly enemies of crows and this arrangement ostensibly enraged the crows to attack. The dead Crow decoy is exceedingly rare.

147

PLATE 162. Snuggler Head Canada Goose by Herters', Inc. Balsa body and cedar head.

PLATE 163. Balsa body Coot decoy by Herters', Inc.

MASON'S DECOY FACTORY

Of all the factory made decoys, the ones made by Mason are the most famous. There are more Mason decoys sitting around in living rooms and collections than any other decoys made in the country. They were in Detroit, going into business around 1895 and continuing until 1924. They made five grades of decoys. The best was labelled "Premier", then came "Challenge", "Detroit" grade (called 3 grade Glass Eye by most collectors), 3rd grade Tack Eye, and Fourth Grade. The last three were called "No. 1 Glass Eye", "No. 2 Glass Eye" and "No. 3 Painted Eye" respectively by the company. There are other names such as "Challenge Grade Hollow" model which was usually a special order.

Weights of all sorts are found on Masons, but there was a standard weight used by Mason. They didn't attach them at the factory but shipped them separate in the same box. The buyers had to attach the weight themselves.

Premier Grade Masons had very fine bill and face carving, including a nicely carved nail at the end of the bill. This nail carving was not present on any of the lesser grades. The nail on the Challenge Grade decoys, for instance, was merely painted on.

Premier Grade characteristics are: finely carved bills with the all important **carved** nail representation; two-piece hollow bodies normally, with flat bottoms; glass eyes, and very beautiful paint, including the well known Mason swirl pattern on the breast.

Challenge Grade Masons are characterized by either solid (most of them) or hollow bodies, depending upon how the hunter ordered them; bill carving not nearly so pronounced as on Premier Grades; good paint but also not quite so elaborate as the Premiers; most significantly, a painted black dot to represent the nail, not carved as in Premiers; and glass eyes.

Standard Grade or **Detroit Grade** Masons have glass eyes; no bill carving at all but details represented by painting. They are all smaller than the Challenge or Premier Grades.

The No. 2 Tack Eye (Mason terminology) is exactly as it says. It is quite nearly the same as the above Standard or Detroit grade but has **tack eyes.**

The No. 3 Painted Eye is the same as the No. 2 except it has painted eyes as stated in the name. This was the most economical grade in the line.

There are a number of non-standard or atypical Masons about, but most of them were special order decoys.

The Mason style of construction and painting was apparently derived from the earlier products of two earlier Michigan factory type decoys made by George Peterson and his successor Jasper N. Dodge (see page <u>142</u>). They were both in business in excess of twenty years prior to the Mason Factory.

Value Ranges for Mason Decoys

Merganser, Brant and Canada Goose decoys have all brought far in excess of the value ranges listed here at various auctions but what is listed here reflects normal averages for decoys in all grades.

Black Duck	$130 - 500
Bluebill	100 - 400
Blue Wing Teal	300 - 700
Brant	400 - 850
Canada Goose	500 - 1250
Canvasback	100 - 350
Goldeneye	100 - 300
Green Wing Teal	300 - 700
Mallard	150 - 500

PLATE 164. A Mason Premier model Canvasback drake. Two-piece hollow body, swirled breast paint, glass eyes, and fine detailed face and bill carving. If you examine the photo carefully, you can just barely see the **carved** nail at the tip of the bill. This is found only on Mason's Premier grade decoys.

PLATE 165. This bottom view of the Canvasback in Plate 164 shows the typical Mason ballast weight and the brand of the Berdan Gun Club.

PLATE 166. This Mason drake Widgeon decoy is a Premier grade model. It exhibits all the Premier grade characteristics although you may not be able to discern the carved nail in the photograph.

PLATE 167. A hen Broadbill in the Challenge grade by Mason. An unusual Challenge grade hollow body decoy.

PLATE 168. Drake Broadbill mate to the decoy in Plate 167. The Challenge grade painted black dot nail representation is clearly seen on the end of the bill. Hollow body.

PLATE 169. A Mason Standard or Detroit grade Greenwing Teal drake. This decoy is not in exceptional shape but it is a species of Mason decoy not found often.

PLATE 170. Standard or Detroit grade Bluewing Teal drake by Mason's Decoy Factory.

PLATE 171. A Challenge grade Mason Brant in excellent condition. This particular decoy was once the property of the Barron Gun Club. The brand is always applied in two places, on the back and on the left side, as seen in the illustration.

PLATE 172. A Mason Standard or Detroit grade Canvasback hen. This solid body decoy is a special order. The body is unusually long and slender for the typical Detroit grade decoys and the head looks more like Goldeneye heads than Canvasback heads.

PLATE 173. This is the drake Canvasback mate to the hen in Plate 172.

PLATE 174. This Premier grade Mason hen Redhead is a special order decoy. It differs primarily from the typical Premier grade in that the tail is not swept up as is usual. There is an unusual cheek profile. It is a Mason but differs considerably from the norm.

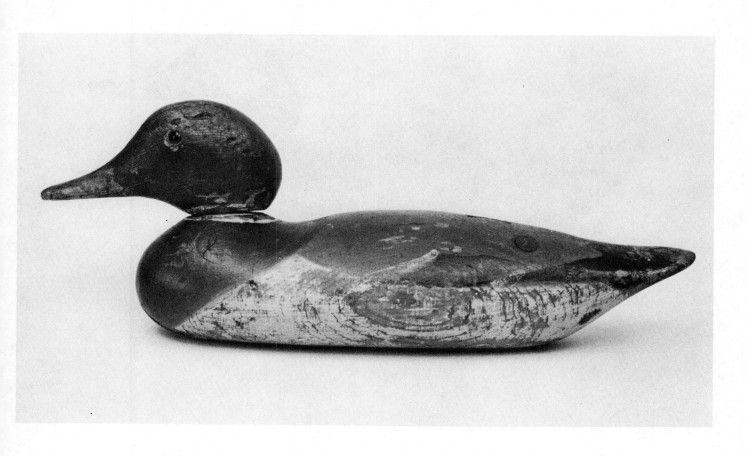

PLATE 175. Mason Standard or Detroit grade Mallard drake.

PLATE 176. Challenge grade Mason Black Duck.

PLATE 177. Very nice Standard or Detroit grade Mason Black Duck.

PLATE 178. Challenge grade Mason Brant.

PLATE 179. Pair of Mason's Decoy Factory Teals. Challenge grade.

WILLIAM E. PRATT MANUFACTURING COMPANY

This company was in business from 1920 in Joliet, Illinois. In 1924, when the Mason's Decoy Factory went out of business, Pratt bought out their production line and went into decoy making full time, but the company never approached the quality of Mason's decoys. Most of their decoys exhibit the rough ridging left by the lathe blades. They called this a "feather finish" model, but this was more likely a way to glamorize their lack of sanding and finishing the decoys.

Because Pratt most likely picked up some Mason inventory with the purchase, collectors sometimes find nice Mason bodies with Pratt heads on them.

The decoy in the accompanying Plate 180 is a typical Mason Premier grade pattern, but obviously not nearly so well finished. The other two are better finished, higher quality Pratt products. They offered various degrees of quality over the years until eventually being purchased by the Animal Trap Company.

PLATE 180. This Bluewing Teal drake is a very good example of the feather finish model made by William E. Pratt Manufacturing Company. This was apparently their way of saying that they didn't send them. See Victor Animal Trap Company on page 166.

PLATE 181. Drake Mallard attributed to the William E. Pratt company. This one may be a re-head, as the head seems out of proportion for the body. This is not the norm for Pratt decoys.

PLATE 182. A nice Bluewing Teal drake attributed to the William E. Pratt Manufacturing Company.

H. A. STEVENS c. 1880

Harvey A. Stevens lived and worked in Weedsport, New York. He died in 1894 and his brother George W. Stevens apparently carried on for a while, for there have been some found with his initials in the brand.

Stevens decoys were marked "H. A. Stevens, Weedsport, N. Y." by use of stencils, so if you find an original paint model, it should be easy to identify. If you are not so lucky, there are other reliable ways. He almost always manufactured his decoys with an inletted lead weight (poured into a drilled circular hole) and a line tie staple recessed in a similar hole. Tails are paddle type and glass eyes were the rule. Paint was fairly thick and the comb feather technique was used extensively and heads were screwed into the body from the top, resulting hole plugged with a piece of dowel.

The collector value range for Stevens decoys is from $300 to $900.

PLATE 183. This Redhead drake was made by H. A. Stevens. The very nicely formed, flattish body and paddle tail are typical of his factory decoys. Note the comb feather paint pattern.

PLATE 184. Bottom view of the Redhead in Plate 183. The one-inch holes with lead in one for ballast (seometimes more than one is found), and the one forward has a staple for the anchor line tie. Both are characteristic of Stevens decoys. If you look very closely, you can see the remnants of his brand. The "H" and "W" are barely discernible above and between the weight and line tie. This part of the brand "H.A. Stevens, Weedsport, N.Y.". Toward the rear end you can see the "S" and "D" from the word "STANDARD".

PLATE 185. An H. A. Stevens Scaup decoy. Note the comb feather painting and the nicely carved mandible details.

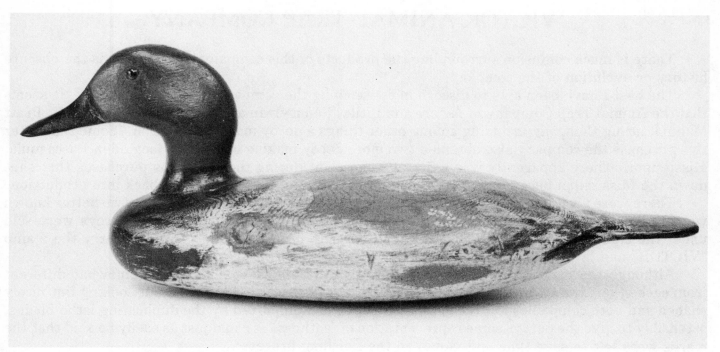

PLATE 186. Typical Canvasback drake by H. A. Stevens.

VICTOR ANIMAL TRAP COMPANY

There is much confusion surrounding the products of this company. The reason is the obscure history or evolution of the company.

The best I have been able to discern in researching the company remains confusing. It seems that the Animal Trap Company of America in Lititz, Pennsylvania, purchased the William E. Pratt Manufacturing Company including among other things a decoy making operation. Some time after this purchase the company also obtained two more decoy making operations located in Pascagoula, Mississippi. There apparently was a fire at some point during these various purchases that shut down the Mississippi decoy operations for a period of time, but they did go back into production.

There were various companies making decoys in the Pascagoula area, but the two better known were those of the Victor Company and the Pascagoula Decoy Company whose decoys were sold under the tradename "PADCO". The Victor Company products, when marked, carry the stamp "VICTOR" and later, "ANIMAL TRAP CO. OF MISSISSIPPI, Inc.".

Although the paint patterns used by the two different companies were somewhat different from each other, the lathe-turned bodies were almost identical. They are crude looking but nicely shaped and both companies left the ribbed or ridged look imparted by the duplicating lathe blades, ostensibly to give the decoys some representation of feathers. It could just as easily be said that the marks were left to save time and money in the finishing process.

The degree to which the grooves or ribs are apparent was probably due to the type of wood from which the decoys were made. Generally speaking, the harder the wood the more obvious the ribbing.

Heads were attached by wooden dowels, some being left loose for changing head position or transporting them without damage.

Painting was done by spraying, perhaps with some hand work. Hundreds of thousands of these birds were made and sold through several companies' sales catalogs, such as Sears and Roebuck and Montgomery Ward. They became tremendously popular after the end of World War II. They are probably the most commonly found decoys in the country so, unless the decoy from one of these companies is a rarely found type, such as a Teal, chances are the value is going to be less than $100.00, even if found in original paint.

PLATE 187. A Victor Animal Trap Company Mallard drake. Note the ridges around the body that were made by the duplicating lathe blades. It has glass eyes, which is the rule with these birds.

PLATE 188. A close-up photograph of the "VICTOR" brand found on the bottom of the Mallard decoy in Plate 187.

WILDFOWLERS DECOYS, INC.

This company began doing business in 1939 in Old Saybrook, Connecticut, and is presently located in Babylon, New York, where it is still in business, laying legitimate claim to being the oldest operating decoy factory in the country.

The early decoys, made in Old Saybrook, all have slightly inletted heads while later model made after the factory was moved (1958) to Quogue, Long Island, New York, were not inletted.

Originally the decoys were made from white pine but after World War II they were made from balsa (excepting a few special order birds). Heads were of cedar, pine or birch, with the latter being most common. All had glass eyes.

One very helpful identifying characteristic is the use of an attractive round brand or trademark. The decoys were not always branded, but when they were the brand bore the name of the town in which the factory was located. Thus, if you encounter a branded decoy, you can easily determine its approximate age.

The collector value range for Wildfowler decoys is from $100 to $500.

PLATE 189. An Atlantic Coast Model Brant decoy made in the Old Saybrook, Connecticut Wildfowler factory. This decoy has a balsa body.

PLATE 190. Redhead drake by Wildfowler Decoys. This bird has a representation of a nail at the end of the bill, not normally found on later models.

PLATE 191. This Wildfowler hen Red Breasted Merganser decoy has glass eyes, a cedar head, and balsa body. It was made in the Quogue, L. I., New York, factory.

PLATE 192. This is a drake Red Breasted Merganser by Wildfowler. It was made in the Quogue, L. I., New York factory and has balsa body, cedar head and glass eyes.

PLATE 193. Closeup photograph of the Wildfowler brand sometimes found on their decoys. This brand remained the same throughout production, with only the factory town location changing. This particular one is from the Quogue, Long Island, factory.

PLATE 194. This Wildfowler brand is from the Old Saybrook, Connecticut factory.

PLATE 195. Wildfowler Decoy Company Black Duck.

PLATE 196. A Canvasback male by Wildfowler. Mint condition, never hunted over.

PLATE 197. A drake Pintail by Wildfowler.

PLATE 198. A hen Scaup made by Wildfowler.

PLATE 199. Drake Scaup by Wildfowler. Mate to the hen Scaup in Plate 198 above.

PLATE 200. A very nice unbranded balsa body Canada Goose made by Wildfowler.
Original paint.

by Carl F. Luckey

This fully illustrated guide lists thousands of items with over 1000 illustrations of lures, reels, etc. Over 200 manufacturers and distributors listed with such names as Al Foss, Arbogast, Creek Chub, Heddon, Keeling, Meisselbach, Moonlight, P & K, Paw Paw, Pflueger, Rush, Shakespeare, Southbend, Truetemper, Vacuum Bait, Winchester, plus hundreds of others. Dating begins pre-1900. One section includes a very helpful group of illustrations showing the configuratons of hardware placement on different baits and the anatomies of reels. The reader will find histories of past and present manufacturers. 8½ x 11, 312 pages, paperback. ISBN 0-89689-018-X.